Alexander the Great

A Captivating Guide to the King Who Conquered the Persian Empire and Babylon, Including His Impact on Ancient Greece and Rome

Free Bonus from Captivating History (Available for a Limited time)

Hi History Lovers!

Now you have a chance to join our exclusive history list so you can get your first history ebook for free as well as discounts and a potential to get more history books for free! Simply visit the link below to join.

Captivatinghistory.com/ebook

Also, make sure to follow us on Facebook, Twitter and Youtube by searching for Captivating History.

Contents

Introduction

There are so many advantages to having a vast, sprawling empire with diverse people groups all under your thumb, a land so big that invaders would refuse to attack it for the simple reason that it would be far too expensive and difficult, not to mention deadly. However, that size comes with a cost. Administration of a huge country is a problem even today, with multiethnic territorial giants such as the United States of America, Russia, Canada, and India constantly facing various issues that threaten their stability. And, of course, this problem is not new. A mere century and a half ago, the United Kingdom held one-tenth of the known world. It was possibly the biggest single empire in human history, and it took merely a few generations for most of those lands to be lost, either to diplomacy or war. The French and Spanish maritime empires suffered a similar fate, as did slightly older empires, such as Austria-Hungary and the Ottomans. Naturally, they would all follow the example of *the* empire, that of the Romans, and indeed, one can draw many parallels between the failures of ancient Rome and those of enormous modern-day multiethnic countries.

But even Rome had a predecessor. At one point, a man appeared in Europe who had decided to conquer all of the Middle East by wrestling power away from the Persians and establishing a huge power base for his kinsmen. One man who would be the not-so-perfect combination of a cunning military general and a raging spoiled brat. One man who would do so much during his life that even today, people write tales and sing songs of his greatness. And he was, indeed, great, to the point where said greatness became his sobriquet. That man was, of course, Alexander of Macedon.

Alexander's life and exploits are fascinating. Few European figures have had such a rich experience when it comes to fighting, conquest, sieging, and slaying, and few would gain it after their death. And as is often the case with such great conquerors, Alexander would remain a controversial figure. Few can fully agree what attributes (and flaws) we can ascribe to the former Macedonian king, but most will agree with the basics—the inheritor of the Macedonian throne had been an exceptional individual, one worthy of further research.

But what kind of a man was Alexander? Did he aspire to what the historians suggest, an idea of Greekness and a single national identity, or was there something else in the works? What was his worldview? How did he treat his allies, both current and former? What about the treatment of his enemies? If those are just some of the questions you might have about Alexander, then you're in luck. This book will serve as a captivating guide into the life of one of Europe's best-known conquerors, following his life from the moment he came into this world to the moment he left it. And though this is a story told and retold a thousand times before, both during antiquity and during our modern times, it is definitely worth retelling it a thousand and one times more.

Statue of Alexander the Great, circa 3ʳᵈ century BCE, Istanbul Archaeology Museum, Turkey[j]

Chapter 1 – The Early Days: Alexander's Childhood and the Mediterranean and Middle Eastern Lands during Philip II's Reign

Alexander's Birth and Lineage

Before moving on with the tale of Alexander, we should first address the dating system used in this book. Everything that happened from the birth of Alexander to the fall of the last of his empire's successor states occurred before the supposed birth of Jesus Christ, i.e., what we today call the Common Era. With that in mind, the years mentioned in this book will go backward. In other words, the year 356 will come after the year 357, not before. Moreover, since they are all before the Common Era, we won't be using the acronym "BCE," as it will be implied.

The future conqueror and military genius of Macedon was probably born around 356 in the then-capital of Pella. His parents were, unsurprisingly, both members of royalty. Incidentally, both would have a massive effect on young Alexander's development, albeit in entirely different ways.

Alexander's mother was called Olympias. Before marrying into the Macedonian royalty, she was the eldest daughter of Neoptolemus I, the king of Epirus. Considering how important she would be in forming Alexander's political and personal opinions going forward, it's instrumental to investigate her origins a bit further. Olympias, who was a Molossian Greek woman, did not originally bear that name. In fact, according to ancient authors like Plutarch, she had a grand total of four names. At first, she was called Polyxena. Right before marrying Alexander's father, she changed her name to Myrtale and later to Olympias (we shall cover the reasons behind this third change later). In her final years, she changed her name again, this time to Stratonice. Changing one's name was common back in the ancient world, especially when it came to members of royal families. In fact, we can see that trend even among the rulers who would end up inheriting Alexander's empire after his death.

Olympias's marriage to Alexander's father was more than likely one of political interest. The Molossian Greeks of Epirus were Macedon's closest neighbors, and after the death of Olympias's father in 360, her uncle, Arymbas, took the throne. To secure his position, Arymbas entered a treaty with the Macedonians, and that treaty was secured with the marriage of Olympias to the current Macedonian ruler. Their marriage took place in 358 when the princess of the Molossians was seventeen years old. That seems like a rather young age by today's standards, but in the ancient Balkans (and most of the ancient world, really), people would marry even younger than that. If anything, seventeen was considered a bit late in life to marry.

The Molossian Greek rulers were a dynasty that supposedly had its roots in legend, with their founding king Neoptolemus (not to be confused with Olympias's father) being the son of the legendary hero Achilles. This supposed heroic lineage would become an important factor in how Alexander saw himself later in life, though Achilles would be far from the only mythical or otherworldly individual whom the future conqueror of the known world would invoke. In fact, part of his pride would come from this supposed heroic ancestry, pride that Alexander's mother would have more than likely possessed as well.

Up to this point, we didn't mention Alexander's father by name, yet his feats were, for the time, incredibly impressive, and for a while, he was one of the most competent (if not outright *the* most competent) rulers in ancient Europe. Philip II was born as the third son of King Amyntas III and Queen Eurydice I. Amyntas was known, at least in tradition, as the ruler who first managed to unify the Macedonians into one country, as the regions of Upper and Lower Macedonia were originally separate. In his youth, Philip would spend several years in captivity, being held in both Illyria and Thebes. His Theban captivity was particularly instrumental, considering that the city-state had dominion over all other Greek states and especially since he had been the student of the notable general Epaminondas and under the care of important Theban public figures such as Pelopidas and Pammenes. By spending time with these people, Philip acquired significant military and diplomatic skills, which he would put to good use as early as 359.

The year 364 saw Philip return to Macedon. The country had been in turmoil for a while by that point. Six years prior to Philip's return, his father had died, and the throne went to his eldest son, Alexander II. However, Alexander would be assassinated soon after in 367, and the throne went to the underage Perdiccas III, though the real power was held by Ptolemy of Aloros. Interestingly, Ptolemy would usurp the throne but remain as Perdiccas's regent until the boy came of age to rule by himself. Perdiccas would later kill Ptolemy and assume the throne, ruling until 360. Perdiccas would lose his life in a battle that year, failing spectacularly to reclaim Upper Macedonia (at the time, the region was briefly conquered by Bardylis, an Illyrian king) and losing a supposed total of four thousand men in the process. Since Perdiccas's son, Amyntas IV, was only six years old, Philip became his regent in 359. And as is often the case in ancient politics, the regent soon usurped the throne and became king.

We will cover more of Philip's exploits in a bit. For now, it's vital to focus on the political situation of both the Balkans and the Middle East during these turbulent times. After all, Philip's Macedon was merely one player in a massive game of political chess, though he was a powerful, cunning, and ruthless player who seemed as if he couldn't lose. In short, he was the perfect interlude for what was to come with the reign of Alexander when Macedon was at its peak.

Silver tetradrachm of Philip II of Macedon, circa 359 BC

The Mediterranean and the Middle East during the Reign of Philip II

Macedon

Macedon was a brutal, autocratic society long before Philip took the crown. For centuries, these rowdy, rough mountain folk had been actively warring with neighboring nations, including the Greeks. Interestingly, most people tend to conflate the two people, claiming that Alexander was a Greek ruler rather than a Macedonian one. On the other side of that spectrum, you have people who claim that the Greeks ceased to exist during the period of Alexander's reign and that they merely assimilated into the larger Macedonian society. In truth, neither of those statements is true. Not only are Greeks and Macedonians separate people, but the Greek side of the argument would go out of its way to differentiate themselves from their northern neighbors. To a Greek citizen of one of their many city-states (or *poleis*, sg. *polis*), the Macedonians were barbarians, i.e., uncouth and uncultured people who were beneath the Greeks. This attitude of barbarians and non-barbarians would start with the Greeks, but it would spread to all other major powers of southern Europe, mainly Rome and the Eastern Roman Empire.

The Macedonians, in turn, did not generally seem to care what the Greeks thought about them, though there were some who considered the two people groups as one. Philip II, in particular, was an extreme proponent of the Pan-Hellenic idea, as he considered himself to be Greek. This attitude would reflect in his later exploits, especially in his final years on the throne. He saw himself as a unifier of all Greeks, and he was ready to literally spill blood in order to prove that fact.

Before Philip, during the previous rulers of the so-called Argead dynasty (which included but also ended with Alexander in power; interestingly enough, his full name and designation at the time would have been Alexander III), Macedon was disunited and largely inconsequential. However, after unification and especially after

Philip's takeover of the throne, Macedon would become the biggest power player in the Balkans. Firstly, Philip made good use of the biggest resources that the country had, which included timber, pitch, and hunting game in the highlands; goats and sheep on the pastures of the foothills and the mountain plateaus; and the grain that was cultivated in the lowlands. Of course, these resources alone couldn't boost the Macedonian economy as much as war. During Philip's conquest of the region, he managed to utterly raze Olynthus in 348, the capital of what was then known as the Chalcidian federal state. When he crushed the Greeks, the king of Macedon claimed their territory and distributed it among the Macedonian aristocracy. Some Greeks who swore loyalty to Philip also got to keep their territories or gain some new ones in the process, provided that they acknowledge Philip as their new king. But interestingly enough, Philip also distributed some Chalcidian land to Macedonian commoners who held no real power before then. Thus, he effectively created a sort of new middle class of nobles that would fight for him in times of need. There's even an anecdote where Alexander, according to the ancient Greek historian Arrian, spoke to the Macedonians and stated that his father brought them from the mountains to the plains, more than likely referring to this particular event.

The conquest of Chalcidian lands resulted in another economic benefit for the people of Macedon. Namely, in the mountainous areas of Chalcidian Thrace, or more precisely at Mount Pangaeum (the modern-day Pangaion Hills in Greece), there were multiple mines rich with gold and silver. Mining these metals made Macedon incredibly powerful and Philip one of the wealthier rulers in the Balkans. In fact, the yield from these mines was said to equate to around one thousand silver talents each year. In ancient times, an Attic talent (also known as the Greek or Athenian talent) was worth around sixty *minae* (a *mina* is a unit of both weight and currency in the Near East, equating to sixty *shekels*), six thousand *drachmae* (a *drachma* is an ancient Greek unit of currency) or thirty-six thousand *oboloi* (with the *obol* being another ancient Greek currency unit), making it one of the most valuable units. In terms of silver content, a talent would contain twenty-six kilograms or fifty-seven pounds of pure silver. In early 2021 CE, the value of a single kilogram of silver fluctuates somewhere around $810. In other words, in just one year, the gold and silver mines of Mount Pangaeum would give Philip II a yield valued at $21,060,000. Of course, this might seem like a huge sum, and by all accounts, it is. However, Philip's yearly earnings can't even compare to, for example, how much the Persian emperor earned or how much Alexander would plunder during his exploits.

Philip wasted no time in establishing Macedon as a regional power. The huge sums of money he had been gaining from the mines alone were more than enough to buy anything he needed, from local Greek supporters to entire armies of mercenaries. Moreover, it was during his time in power that the biggest shift in Macedonian society came, considering that the majority of people were simple farmers or herdsmen. And while Philip didn't manage to fully convert Macedon to a Hellenic country complete with Greek customs and cultural mores, he had definitely given the country a new prestige. And with that prestige also came all of the shortcomings of existing Hellenic cultures, especially the idea that Macedon was now cultured and that every other nation, save the Greeks, was barbaric.

Greek States

During Macedon's ascension, the once glorious Greek cities were in a state of disarray. Not long before, Sparta had crushed Athens in the Peloponnesian War (431–404). However, Sparta would not keep its hegemony over the other city-states it had beaten. In fact, when Sparta sought to conquer what were once parts of the Athenian maritime "empire," Athens would rise up and join with another powerful ally who was snubbed by the Spartans: Thebes. Around the year 386, Spartan King Agesilaus II would actually come to an agreement with Persian Great King Artaxerxes II that resulted in a series of so-called "common peaces." According to them, Persia would guarantee the safety, security, and autonomy of the mainland

Greek cities. However, this agreement came with a price. Namely, there were lots of Greeks who were living in Asia Minor at the time. As per the agreement, Sparta had to abandon these Greeks to the fate of the Persian king and the Persian satraps that were ruling the nearby regions (a satrap is a kind of provincial governor in ancient Persia, a title that nearly all future Persian rulers would retain for their subordinates, and yes, that title survived when Alexander came to power). The Persians were still seen as the archnemeses of all Greeks, so having any kind of treaty with them, whether it was prudent or not political, could have been (and was) construed as treason to the Greek people. But even that act alone would not tip Sparta's Greek enemies over the edge. That tipping point came when the Spartans occupied Thebes in 382 and placed a garrison upon the city's acropolis (a citadel or a fortification that made up the highest point of an ancient Greek city).

Sparta yielded its power to the combined strengths of Thebes and Athens in 379 when the two managed to expel Spartan soldiers from the city's territory. The very next year, Thebes reestablished the Boeotian League, an alliance of independent cities hostile to the Spartans. It had been formed well before the Peloponnesian War and got its name from the so-called Boeotarchs (chief ministers of war and foreign affairs that the city-states would elect to represent them, a title that came to prominence after 379). One of the key aspects of this Theban restoration of the Boeotian League was army reform, which included 150 pairs of gay lovers called the Sacred Band of Brothers. Pelopidas would lead this band of warriors, while the overall military and strategical organization fell under Epaminondas. Those would be the same people who would hold Philip II hostage during his tender years and the same people he would learn from the most.

Epaminondas was indeed a skilled general and statesman. His biggest claim to fame was in 371 at the famed Battle of Leuctra against Spartan King Cleombrotus I. It would be here that Epaminondas applied a different sort of military tactic that would utterly crush the

Spartan army, killing most of its elite fighters and taking down the Spartan king along the way. Similar tactics found their way to Macedon, with both Philip and Alexander implementing them during their military exploits. The Battle of Leuctra was the single biggest defeat of Sparta in decades, if not centuries, and it was the deciding factor as to who would take charge of the Hellenic world at the time.

But Epaminondas wasn't done yet. In 370, he would make his way into the very heartland of the Peloponnesus (Peloponnese), the territory known as Arcadia, where he even founded a new capital city of Megalopolis. Not only did he hold power over the Spartans on their own home turf, but he had also deprived them of their slaves (the helots) and made sure the Peloponnesian League, which had been formed by the Spartans in their heyday, fell to the wayside by forming his own Arcadian League. In short, Epaminondas was one of the principal reasons behind Thebes's rise to power in the 360s.

Sadly, Thebes would not maintain that power. In the mid-360s, their relationship with Athens became strained again, crushing any potential of Thebes having hegemony over the other Greek *poleis*. The main deciding factor of the crushing of Thebes was, in fact, another famed battle that took place in 362, the Battle of Mantinea. Technically, it was meant to be a stand-off between Thebes and Sparta, with King Agesilaus II leading the Spartans and Epaminondas in charge of the Thebans. Of course, Thebes did not fight alone, as it had both the Boeotian League and the so-called Arcadian League on their side. The latter league was an alliance of the Arcadian city-states that was formed by Thebes in order to maintain control over the region. Interestingly, the Spartans were joined by Athens, their old enemy, in an alliance against Epaminondas, as did the two minor Peloponnesian city-states of Elis and Mantinea. Mantinea was, at some point, a part of the Arcadian League, but it broke off after Thebes had seized control of a Pan-Hellenic sanctuary of Zeus, located in the small town of Olympia in Elis. This, consequently, would have been a good enough reason for Elis to go to war with the Arcadian League, but it was already in open conflict with the league; the Eleans had a well-known territorial grudge against the Arcadians. In other words, all of Thebe's opponents had a good reason to see Thebes fail, save for Athens. To them, it was simply an opportunity to take Thebes down a peg and prevent them from having total control.

The Battle of Mantinea held other levels of importance for the Greeks as well. It was here that Sparta crushed Athens during the Peloponnesian War in 418 in what was to be the largest land-based battle of the conflict. The Spartans were the winners here, and the war resulted in the defeat of Athens and the Mantineans rejoining the Spartan-led Peloponnesian League, which they had abandoned in favor of Athens. In short, Mantinea was a painful reminder of two major defeats for both Athens and Mantinea, as well as a place of former victory that contemporary Sparta had to emulate to regain its old status as a power. It didn't help that the allies against Thebes used to be bitter enemies on the battlefield and had to choose the lesser evil simply to thwart a potential hegemon.

But the prelude to the battle was nothing compared to what happened during and especially after. Epaminondas's troops had actually crushed the Spartan-led alliance, despite both sides claiming victory. It was a stark reminder that Sparta was no longer the juggernaut it once was, and it was an indicator of how unprepared Athens was to exert any kind of authority over the Greek *poleis*. However, Epaminondas himself was mortally wounded and would succumb to those wounds soon after. Moreover, the men he designated to succeed him in all affairs of the state, Iolaidas and Daiphantus, both died during the battle as well. And while the Mantineans also lost their commander to the fight and had to retreat, the Theban victory over the frail Spartan alliance was far from beneficial. Had Pyrrhus of Epirus been born around this time, the term "Pyrrhic victory" would have applied to this end result perfectly.

After the battle was over, both sides sued for peace. The disunion of the Greek states had deteriorated the region and left thousands dead or dying. Not only did the Greeks not have a unified country (something that would have fit the growing notion of Greekness that was prevalent at the time), but their bickering also left them open for attack from another outside aggressor, and it just so happened to be barbarian folk led by the same man who had to serve Epaminondas and Pelopidas all those years ago.

Persia

If there was one cause that could, theoretically, unite all Greeks, if only briefly, it was their joint distaste for Persia. To an average ancient Greek citizen, Persians were the definition of barbarians. However, in terms of history, social organization, and hierarchical stratification, the Persians were far from backwater or underdeveloped. In fact, during the majority of antiquity before the Common Era, the area that would comprise Persia (the modern-day Middle East) would always be home to a massive empire. The Persia of Alexander's time was still under the rule of the original founding dynasty, that of the Achaemenids. Like all major dynasties, the ancestry of the Persian rulers is questionable at best, with the supposed founder of the dynasty, Achaemenes, probably being a minor ruler from either Parsua or Anshan, both minor tribal kingdoms within the Zagros Mountains and both linked to Achaemenes's supposed son, King Teispes. Teispes was, in turn, the supposed father of King Cyrus I and the great-grandfather of King of Kings Cyrus II, also known as Cyrus the Great. His greatness would reflect in the fact that he would be the first to conquer vast regions around his empire, incorporating huge swathes of territory with dozens of different languages, cultures, and beliefs. Moreover, he was the first ruler of the Achaemenids whom we have proper historical records of, as well as the first to style himself with the title "King of Kings," one that would be used by all other Achaemenid rulers until their downfall.

Though as great as Cyrus's empire was, it paled in comparison to the one of his descendant, that of the equally skilled King of Kings Darius I, who ruled from 522 to 486. His empire encompassed all of Asia Minor, huge swathes of the Arabian Peninsula, and most of the Middle East, stretching all the way to the Hindu Valley, both Upper and Lower Egypt, and even major sections of the Balkans.

Darius and his son, who would later become King Xerxes I, who ruled from 486 to 465, would both be directly involved in Greek affairs, with each of them starting an invasion of the Balkans. And while both would initially have streaks of victories over the Greeks, they would usually be bested and forced to retreat or halt the invasion. For Darius, the key battle he lost in his invasion of Greece was the famed Battle of Marathon in 490, while for Xerxes, it was two conflicts: the Battle of Salamis in 480 and the Battle of Plataea in 479.

All of these events took place long before Philip became king and the birth of Alexander, but they underline a particular trend that continued to play a significant role in contemporary politics of the city-states. The general opinion of Persians among the ancient Balkan people, aside from viewing them as barbarians, was that they were a powerful enemy but that they could be defeated. All the Greeks needed to do was unite and see defeating the Persians as a common cause, a notion that orators of the time, like Isocrates, spoke of at length. Naturally, with the state of disarray that was sweeping the city-states, no potential alliance amongst themselves was going to happen. And bizarrely enough, there were times when the Greeks actually fought for the Persians, albeit as mercenaries. The most noteworthy example would be that of Xenophon and the Ten Thousand, a Greek mercenary unit that Cyrus the Younger, a satrap and a prince, employed to try to wrestle power from his brother, King of Kings Artaxerxes II, in the final years of the 5th century BCE.

Fortunately for the disunited Greek *poleis* during the time of Philip II, though Persia was still a strong opponent, it was nowhere near as powerful as it was during the rule of King Darius I. The very last ruler of the Achaemenids, King of Kings Darius III, still held autocratic power over the people despite being arguably the weakest ruler of the dynasty, though his country was divided into twenty satrapies (territories administered by a satrap) for easy governance. Born under the name of Artashata, the future king would rise to prominence as a soldier under King of Kings Artaxerxes III when, during a particular military expedition, he killed a man in single combat. He became the satrap of Armenia and soon after was recorded as being the vassal of Artaxerxes III. Interestingly, he would become king through a series of court intrigues and assassinations, all involving the same man, a court eunuch named Bagoas. Acting as a vizier, Bagoas orchestrated the poisoning of Artaxerxes III and the majority of his sons in late 338, save for two. The youngest of them, Arses, would be crowned as Artaxerxes IV, with Bagoas playing a major role in his ascension. It was this assassination and abrupt shift in power that historians believe led to the downfall of the Achaemenid dynasty, which, in turn, made Alexander's conquest of the Persian Empire all the easier. The following eight years would be some of the most turbulent for the Persians, as Artaxerxes IV tried to wrestle power and influence away from Bagoas, including trying to have him poisoned. Bagoas, however, survived, and he orchestrated another poisoning of the new King of Kings in 336, killing the very man he first placed on the throne. In choosing the next king, Bagoas went with seasoned Artashata, himself a distant relative of the Achaemenid kings and a popular choice among the aristocracy. Rather expectedly, Bagoas tried poisoning Darius as well, but according to contemporary sources, the new King of Kings was warned in advance, which prompted him to confront the eunuch and force him to drink the poison himself.

Court intrigue and the constant shift of those in power were not new to the Persians, but things were developing rather rapidly, and there's no denying that Darius III had inherited a crumbling empire. With his own office not particularly secure and the Greeks in the Balkans becoming disunited, a power vacuum of sorts was slowly forming, one that would also be felt in other parts of the ancient world (notably in Egypt, which at the time was under Persian dominion). It's a power vacuum that Philip II intended to utilize, one that would bring Macedon to the forefront as the newest major power player in the Middle East.

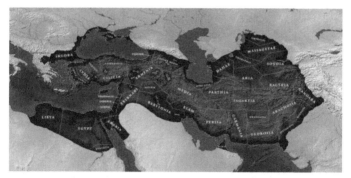

Map of the Achaemenid Empire at its peak during the reign of Darius I, circa 480 BCE[ii]

Alexander's Childhood

As the heir apparent of Philip II, young Alexander was appropriately brought up as a fledging prince at the court of Pella. The first person to raise him was a nurse called Lanike, whose brother was Cleitus the Black, one of Alexander's future generals. When Alexander came of age, he received two tutors: Leonidas (a kinsman to Olympias and an incredibly stern teacher) and Lysimachus of Acarnania. It would be some years before the famed philosopher, Aristotle, would become the tutor to the young heir apparent, so most of Alexander's formative years were left to the aforementioned pair of tutors, as well as Olympias herself.

Alexander was taught the basics of literacy, numeracy, and physical exercise. Like all Macedonian princes before him, he was also taught how to hunt, ride a horse, play the lyre, and fight. It was also during these tender years (possibly when he was around twelve years old) that Alexander first acquired his famed horse, a rowdy steed whom he named Bucephalas (literally "ox-head"). There are legends about how Alexander got Bucephalas, but they cannot be historically verified as fact. We will go over some of the more prominent myths about Alexander's life in Chapter 6.

It might be worth noting that Philip was away for most of Alexander's life, more often than not campaigning abroad and consolidating his kingdom. This left the task of raising Alexander to the court officials and his mother. As such, the young prince became heavily influenced by those who taught him. Olympias would be his dearest and most trusted advisor during this period, and a lot of her personal philosophy and beliefs became part of Alexander's own outlook on life. It's not a stretch to say that the young heir apparent was far more attached to his mother than to Philip, a fact that might have even influenced other events in his life. But Olympias wasn't the only person to have such a strong impact on the young prince. As his chief tutor, Aristotle would be an incredibly important individual in Alexander's life, so much so that there are reports of Alexander sending specimens of plants and animals back to his old mentor in Europe during his conquests, for the philosopher had sparked the young conqueror's interest for biology, zoology, and botany. More than anything, Aristotle encouraged Alexander to study Greek literature and history, so the young king famously had an annotated copy of the *Iliad* everywhere he went, with the annotations made by Aristotle himself.

Aristotle would definitely be Alexander's most important teacher, but he would not be the last. In fact, Alexander had up to thirteen different tutors in total over the course of his youth. One of his personal favorites, other than Aristotle, was Anaximenes of

Lampsacus, a historian and rhetorician of some renown. He would end up accompanying the young ruler during his conquest of the Middle East and would end up writing historical works on both the young prince and his father. Alexander valued Anaximenes's opinion highly, which does underline one important character trait that we will touch more upon in a future chapter. Namely, despite not being a scholar himself (and despite favoring war and conquest over learning), Alexander would hold learned men in high regard and would go out of his way to keep earning their respect.

Finally, it should be noted that during Alexander's tender years, he would strike up friendships with people who would become key players in his new empire. Aristotle did teach him, but Alexander was far from his only pupil. In fact, there was an entire group of individuals that Aristotle taught, and they all convened at the ancient Temple of the Nymphs in the old town of Mieza (near modern Lefkadia). More than a few of these pupils would become Alexander's generals and close confidants. The most famous of these would, without a doubt, be Hephaestion, who was by far Alexander's closest companion and possible lover and who would follow the young king throughout his conquest. Other future generals of Alexander that he met at Mieza included Ptolemy I Soter, Cassander, Lysimachus, and Cleitus the Black.

But it wasn't just at Mieza that future adherents of Alexander would meet the young prince. In fact, some of the other prominent figures during his time of conquest, such as Harpalus, Nearchus, Erigyius, and Laomedon, all met Alexander around this time but not as pupils of Aristotle. More importantly, save for Harpalus, they were all Greek. This might not be an important detail to consider overall, considering how multiethnic Alexander's empire would be, but having so many Greek natives as generals in his future army (or people in high positions of power) was an indicator of at least some level of Pan-Hellenism on Alexander's part. After all, the Greeks did not consider Macedonians to be any more civilized or less barbaric than, say, the

Persians. And despite there being Greek companions of Alexander who would win their fair share of the spoils during the conquest, the attitude among the Greeks toward the Macedonians did not change.

Interestingly enough, Alexander's future entourage did not simply consist of Macedonians and Greeks, two people groups that rarely saw eye to eye. In fact, in his early teens, Alexander would also come to know a few important Persians as well, individuals who more than likely gave both Philip and the young prince inside information on the troubles at the Persian court. One such key figure was Artabazos II. A high-ranking official at the court of King of Kings Artaxerxes II, Artabazos would become the satrap of Lesser Phrygia (an area in Asia Minor directly southeast of the Dardanelles) after fighting against a Cappadocian insurgent known as Datames who had joined other satraps in the Great Satraps' Revolt (366–360); incidentally, Artabazos's own brother, Ariobarzanes, who held the satrapy of Lesser Phrygia before Artabazos, would also join the revolt against the king. And though Artabazos himself lost, the revolt was squashed, and King Artaxerxes II gave the general the position his crucified brother once occupied.

Sadly, Artabazos would not hold that position long, as he would rebel against the new king, Artaxerxes III, in 356. After a series of conflicts and battles, a huge portion of which involved Artabazos employing the services of Greek mercenaries, he was forced into exile, choosing to take himself and his extended family to the court of none other than Philip II in 352. Over the course of the next decade, he would become well acquainted with court life, becoming close with young Alexander. Artabazos's own daughter, Barsine, spent the majority of her adolescent years at the Macedonian court. While largely inconsequential during this period, Barsine would be a key figure more than a decade after Alexander's death as a supposed mother of his illegitimate son Heracles. While she definitely knew and was probably close with the young prince, it's more than likely that they were never lovers.

Artabazos would not be the only individual from Persia to become one of Alexander's close confidants, however. Two additional people, Amminapes of Parthia and a man named Sisines, would also join the Macedonian court at roughly the same time as Artabazos. However, there is some debate as to how they joined. With Amminapes, it was pretty cut and dry, as he had fled Persia alongside Artabazos as a rebel against King Artaxerxes III. Sisines, on the other hand, might have either been in the same revolt, or he could have come as an ambassador of the satrapy of Egypt. Either way, both men would be key figures in Alexander's life but for entirely different reasons.

Finally, one other individual of note who would play a major role in Alexander's conquest was a statesman and general named Antipater. Antipater, the father of Alexander's friend Cassander, was sixty-four years old when the young prince would be crowned king, having served for many decades under Philip II. Antipater's expertise and prowess made him an important part of Alexander's elite companions despite his advanced age, and he would come to rule as the regent of Macedon while Alexander was away on his conquest. Notably, Antipater was the one who advised Alexander not to depart on his conquest before producing an heir to the throne first, a piece of advice that went unheeded and would result in centuries of catastrophic power struggles and bloodshed.

L'ÉDUCATION D'ALEXANDRE PAR ARISTOTE

Aristotle teaching Alexander, engraving by Charles Laplante, originally published in Louis Figuier's Vie des savants illustres - Savants de l'antiquité (tome 1), *Paris, 1866*

Chapter 2 – Early Reign of Alexander: Coming to the Throne, Consolidating the Greeks, and First Victories on the Battlefield

Coming to the Throne

Alexander would have his first taste of power sometime between 340 and 339 when, at the age of sixteen, he was made regent of Macedon by Philip. The king was going on a campaign that would have him besiege cities such as Byzantium (the future location of Constantinople, modern-day Istanbul, Turkey) and Perinthus, which were both a part of ancient Thrace at the time. The Thracians and Scythians were the most prominent threats to Macedon, although, during Philip's reign, they presented more of a nuisance that had to be dealt with, and they inhabited territories that were ripe for the taking. This territory was on the shores of the Sea of Marmara (known as Propontis then), on the very edge of Asia Minor and, consequently, the Persian Empire. The crumbling empire, which was under Artaxerxes III at the time, would fail to adequately address the growing threat of Philip's troops, a mistake that another people group much closer to Macedon was also making. Namely, with the Sea of Marmara effectively under Philip's control during his siege of the two Thracian cities, two key trade routes that went through the Bosporus and Dardanelle straits were under heavy risk. The Athenians used these trade routes to import their annual supply of wheat from the lands in modern-day Ukraine and Crimea, i.e., lands that had access to the Black Sea. Any type of passage-blocking would result in Athens starving for a year. For that reason, the statesmen of Athens, especially the famed orator Demosthenes, clamored that Athens and its allies should turn their attention from their Persian and Greek enemies to Philip. In fact, Demosthenes would become one of Philip's biggest detractors, and his disdain for Macedon would extend to Philip's son.

However, all of this political turmoil had yet to escalate when Philip was away campaigning and Alexander held the reins of power in Pella. As a means of proving himself, the sixteen-year-old regent would lead a force against a Thracian tribe called Maedi. The Maedi, who occupied a small land area along the Strymon River (the modern-day Struma in Bulgaria), had revolted against the Macedonians while Philip was absent farther east. Alexander took his army and crushed the rebellion with relative ease, forcing the Maedi out of their land. In turn, the young regent populated the area with Greeks and founded his first city, Alexandropolis. This was a practice already employed by his father on at least two separate occasions, and it would be far from the last time that Alexander would found a city bearing his name.

Interestingly enough, Philip did not manage to besiege either Byzantium or Perinthus, making these two of the only real military failures of his reign. However, this did not stop him from proceeding to tamper with Greek interests. As early as 339, Philip managed to seize an entire fleet carrying grain to the Athenian port of Peiraeus. Soon after, the people of the city of Amphissa began to work lands near the temple of Delphi, lands that were sacred to the god Apollo and whose cultivation was equivalent to sacrilege. While Philip was handling this affair, he ordered his son to handle preparations of possibly invading southern Greece. During all of that, Illyrian tribes began to invade Macedon, but Alexander intercepted their attack with speed and ferocity.

Not long after, Philip would lead a march through Thessaly, avoiding the famed Hot Gates of Thermopylae. After entering the region of Phocis, the same region that Delphi was in, Philip would besiege the second-most important city there, Elatea. The importance of this event is reflected in the fact that Elatea was an equal distance away from both Athens and Thebes, meaning that Philip could invade either at any point and that both were in immediate danger of fighting Macedon. Demosthenes, who was proven right by Philip's actions, employed all of his efforts into convincing not only Athens to fight Philip but also Thebes. The Thebans ultimately did join Athens (despite getting offers from Philip's camp as well), and it was only a matter of time before this union would face the massive invading force from the north.

Before the conflict came to pass, Philip marched to Amphissa and conquered it. On his way there, he was met with mercenaries that Demosthenes had hired and captured them. In a last effort to avoid any conflict, upon his return to Elatea, Philip wrote a letter to his opponents, suing for peace. It was rejected, and war was inevitable.

The Battle of Chaeronea and the League of Corinth

Chaeronea, now a modest village in Greece, used to be an ancient city and a member of the Boeotian League, as well as the birthplace of the famed historian and philosopher Plutarch, known for (among other things) his biography of Alexander. Throughout its history, the town would be the site of several different historical battles, but none would rival the one of 338, where Macedon would clash with the union of Greek cities and where both Philip and Alexander demonstrated just how capable they really were.

According to some early sources, both the Macedonians and the Greeks had a force of roughly thirty thousand men. The Greeks were led by Athens and Thebes, though the alliance itself included Troezen, Megara, Epidaurus, Chalcis, Corinth, and Achaea; interestingly enough, Sparta didn't send any troops. On the other hand, the armies of Philip and Alexander consisted mostly of Macedonians, though some Greek generals did fight for Philip.

The exact details of the battle are still a matter of debate among scholars, with most agreeing that Philip commanded the right wing of his troops' formation, while an eighteen-year-old Alexander and some of Philip's most seasoned generals commanded the left wing. And though sources speak of various events, like the total destruction of the Sacred Band of Brothers, they all agree on the outcome. This was, without a doubt, a complete and total victory for Philip and a crushing defeat of the Greek states. After this battle, no Greek union would ever come to pass against Philip, nor could any one city-state take control over the peninsula again.

The aftermath of the battle included an interesting set of events. While Philip did brutally punish those individuals who were against him before and during the Battle of Chaeronea (most notably, Theban leaders who went up against him), he wasn't particularly punitive toward the city-states. In fact, he never wanted to destroy any of them to begin with. After all, he needed a strong coalition that could rival Persia, and destroying each city one by one would be not only counterproductive to that goal but also time-consuming. Most cities simply surrendered to Philip when he marched into them, and he would treat them leniently, rebuilding temples, city walls, and other important buildings, as well as freeing slaves and releasing certain political opponents and war hostages without any ransoms. He did dissolve the Second Athenian League, but the Boeotian League remained in one piece. Both would prove to be inconsequential, considering what he did later.

As we stated earlier, Sparta did not join any side during the conflict. Sparta's goal was to attack its Peloponnesian neighbors while Philip was busy handling the other city-states, but before the Spartans could do any serious damage, Philip razed most of Laconia, leaving Sparta intact.

Young Alexander was a direct participant in the Battle of Chaeronea. This was, in a way, Philip's direct test of his son's military and strategic prowess, and it appears as if the young heir apparent passed with flying colors. He would accompany his father through most of this campaign, even joining him during the ride to the Peloponnesus.

In 337, while in Corinth, Philip made one major move that sealed his position as the undisputed ruler of the Greeks. In this state, the host city of the biennial Isthmian Games (held both before and after the Olympic Games), the king of Macedon would establish his own alliance, the aptly named League of Corinth, which was modeled after all the other leagues mentioned earlier (Athenian, Boeotian, Arcadian, Peloponnesian, etc.). He would act as the league's master, a hegemon, while all other city-states had an obligation to send delegates as members of a permanent council, or synedrion. And indeed, one of Philip's first acts as the hegemon was to conclude a series of bilateral treaties with every single member state of the league.

Philip had a very good reason for concluding all of those treaties and for forming the League of Corinth in the first place. It's also not a coincidence that he did so in Corinth itself. As stated, the city was the host to the Isthmian Games; it was during this particular festival in 481, a whopping 144 years before Philip's founding of the League of Corinth, that the Sparta-led Congress at the Isthmus of Corinth took place, and it was here that a handful of Greek city-states formed the Hellenic League, swearing an oath to fight the Persians and their King of Kings Xerxes I. This symbolism was not lost on Philip, nor on the Greek and Macedonian men who were there (and, more than likely, not on Alexander himself either, considering his own interest in history and later penchant for similar theatrical displays of on-the-nose symbolism).

An Inheritance in Trouble

Young Alexander would not swiftly ascend his father's throne. Around the time of the Battle of Chaeronea (possibly in 337 when he returned to Pella), Philip would marry his seventh wife, Cleopatra, whom he would later rename Cleopatra Eurydice of Macedon. And indeed, that name should ring a few bells, but we will cover that in Chapter 7. Now, Philip marrying a seventh wife was nothing new. The king of Macedon had been known for practicing polygamy, which actually made him stand out from most of the monogamous rulers who came before him. However, Cleopatra Eurydice was the niece of one of his generals, Attalus, who was a Lower Macedonian by birth. In other words, if Philip were to have a son with Cleopatra Eurydice, he would take precedence over Alexander as the next king of Macedon. After all, Alexander was only half-Macedonian since Olympias was Molossian by birth.

It was around this time that Alexander and Olympias fled from Pella. The most commonly cited reason for this exile was supposedly Alexander's reaction to Attalus proclaiming that the gods should give Philip a legitimate heir through his marriage with Cleopatra. While away from his throne, Alexander sought refuge in Illyria, having first left his mother in the city of Dodona in the safety of her brother, King Alexander I of Epirus. It's interesting to see Alexander seeking refuge in Illyria of all places, considering he had defeated them in battle, which would prompt them to think of him as their enemy. Nevertheless, he spent about half a year in Illyria before he eventually came back to the Macedonian court, having worked things out with his father. In all likelihood, Philip never intended to prevent his capable son from inheriting the throne. Alexander might have had a temperament to him, but he was still a military tactical genius and a cunning warrior.

Of course, this would not be the only event that would force a wedge between father and son. In early 336, Pixodarus, a satrap of Caria, spoke to Philip about offering his daughter's hand in marriage to Alexander. Philip refused, instead choosing that the satrap's daughter marry Alexander's older and possibly slightly mentally challenged half-brother, later called Philip III Arrhidaeus. Alexander was persuaded by his mother and his compatriots that Philip planned on making Arrhidaeus his heir through this action, which prompted Alexander to act. He sent Thessalus, an actor and a future close companion, to visit Pixodarus, where the actor told the satrap that his daughter should not marry an illegitimate son but rather the future king of Macedon.

Philip found out about what Alexander did, and his punishment was swift. He exiled four of Alexander's close friends—Nearchus, Harpalus, Erigyius, and Ptolemy—and ordered that Thessalus be brought to him in chains. Philip would go on to tell Alexander that the reason behind him refusing the satrap's offer was the fact that he wanted a better wife for Alexander.

Philip's Death

In the summer of 336, Philip and Alexander were both in Aegae, the ancient capital of Macedon. They were attending the wedding of Cleopatra, Philip's and Olympias's daughter (thus, Alexander's only full sister), and Olympias's brother (thus, eerily enough, Cleopatra's maternal uncle), the aforementioned King Alexander of Epirus. At the wedding, Philip would be assassinated by Pausanias of Orestis, one of his personal bodyguards. Most of Alexander's and Philip's biographers claim that personal vengeance was the motive behind the murder, with a particularly complex set of events leading up to it. Namely, Philip had a supposed love affair with Pausanias of Orestis, which had ended at some point, after which the king of Macedon started a new affair with a different man also named Pausanias; this lover used to be intimate with none other than Attalus, Philip's general and father of his future wife. Evidently, Pausanias of Orestis somehow influenced the other Pausanias to effectively kill himself, which prompted Attalus to get Orestis drunk and rape him out of vengeance. Apparently, Pausanias's vengeance toward Philip stemmed from the fact that the king of Macedon not only didn't punish Attalus but also proclaimed that he would marry his daughter. Of course, none of these stories can be verified, and there are some timing issues when comparing all of the ancient sources. In other words, Pausanias's assassination of Philip could have been entirely politically motivated. In fact, he might have even been put up to it by Alexander and Olympias, as some historians argue.

No matter what the case may be, Philip II of Macedon died in 336. The army and the Macedonian nobles almost immediately proclaimed the young Alexander as king. He was twenty years old when he ascended to the throne, so he was far from being the youngest ruler to ever do so in history, but he was still relatively inexperienced in the matters of ruling.

Consolidating the Greeks

With him now bearing the crown, Alexander spared no time in taking care of his political opponents. The first person he had to get rid of was Amyntas IV. As effective as Philip was as king during his life, he was still technically only a regent for Amyntas during his youth, and though the Macedonian people might not have cared much about Amyntas, especially after having known Philip's prowess in governing and both his and Alexander's prowess in battle, the twenty-nine-year-old noble was still a member of the main Argead family line. In other words, he was still a threat to Alexander's throne. Interestingly enough, Philip didn't see the young ruler as a threat, having given Amyntas his daughter Cynane's hand in marriage (the two would even go on to have a child together, a daughter named Eurydice). However, Alexander didn't share his father's opinion of his cousin and had him killed almost immediately when he came to power.

Amyntas was not the only person whom the new king of Macedon had removed in such a brutal way. Not long after, Alexander would also have two more princes of Macedon killed, minor members of nobility from the region of Lyncestis known as Heromenes and Arrhabaeus, on the suspicion that they were behind the assassination plot of the late King Philip. He did spare the youngest of these princes, known as Alexander Lyncestes, and even considered him a friend and raised him to high honors. Most historians agree that he did this because Lyncestes had sworn fealty to him as king before anyone else did.

However, the early murders that Alexander's new regime would be most infamous for included three of Philip's closest confidants at the time. The first two were Philip's new wife (and, with the ascension of Alexander, his new widow), Cleopatra Eurydice, and her daughter by Philip, Europa. Interestingly, Alexander was not the one who had them killed; it was his mother, Olympias. She had both the mother and the daughter burned alive. Alexander, on the other hand, ordered the death of his father's general and close confidant, Attalus. During Philip's demise, Attalus was in Asia Minor with another military commander, a man called Parmenion. Rumors spread that Demosthenes, in an effort to thwart Alexander and disrupt the Macedonians, sent a letter to Attalus, urging him to rebel against Alexander in exchange for the military backing of Athens. And while that claim is far from verified, it would definitely make sense if it did happen; Attalus and Parmenion had a huge army in Asia Minor, so if they were to rebel against Alexander, they would have the means to at least defend themselves. However, Attalus proved loyal to Alexander, letting the young king know about the letter. This act, though a sign of trust and loyalty, still did not persuade Alexander to let Attalus live. Even if he wasn't in cahoots with the Athenians, he was still a popular general in Asia Minor, so an uprising would definitely cause a problem. Parmenion also knew that, which prompted him to take Attalus's life the same year that Philip (and many other Macedonian nobles, it appears) was killed.

Alexander's new position did not earn him any favors with the local Greek populace. Demosthenes, a fervent opponent of Philip, derided Alexander as a boy and a fool, thinking him inconsequential and unfit to rule. And though this might sound like a judgment on Demosthenes's part, he had very good reason to dismiss Alexander, and most of the Greek nobles agreed with the orator. They might have outright hated Philip due to his barbaric roots and the fact that he had been beating them for years in various battles, but they knew well how ingenious of a general and statesman the late king really was. In comparison, Alexander struck them as a spoiled brat with zero real experience. Of course, it's also highly likely that the Greeks simply didn't know enough about the young king to make a proper assessment.

What they did see, however, was an opportunity. With Philip dead, Greeks from all corners of the peninsula were preparing for a revolt. Athens, Thebes, and Thessaly all rebelled, and there was even news of the Thracian tribes' uprising in the north. Alexander made short work of them. He first marched into Thessaly, routing the rebel army and forcing them to surrender and acknowledge him as king. His very next step was going to Corinth, where Athens, much like Thessaly before it, surrendered to the young conqueror. It would be in Corinth that Alexander would take on the title of hegemon and rule the League of Corinth like his father before him. Furthermore, this was when he was considering taking on Persia, a task his father never did complete.

Of course, Alexander's problems were far from over. As soon as he was done with the Greeks, he marched north to suppress an attack from the Illyrians and the Tribali, two people groups who had been at odds with the Macedonians for a long time. Alexander would go on to crush both in early 335, most notably during his siege of the settlement of Pelium (Pelion in modern Albania). Pelium was an important pass that the Illyrians had been using to enter Macedonian territory, and as such, it was a point that Alexander had to control for his own nation's safety. Furthermore, if he were to be cut off from this pass, he wouldn't be able to reach the Greek city-states, which were already in revolt while the young king was campaigning. In other words, Pelium had to be taken one way or another, and Alexander chose one of the best methods possible—a mix of guerilla tactics and a surprise nighttime attack.

During Alexander's time fighting in the Balkans, Demosthenes managed to convince the people of both Athens and Thebes that the young king had died in battle, even producing a bloodstained messenger as evidence. The Greeks bought this lie and started rebelling against the Macedonians. Interestingly enough, this all-Greek revolt had the monetary backing of none other than Darius III of Persia. Considering Philip's achievements and the close proximity of the Greeks to the Persian borders, the King of Kings was well informed on Alexander's plan to attack his land, so he was more than eager to fuel a rebellion with money that might end the Macedonian plans of conquest. Demosthenes himself had reportedly been receiving a substantial amount of money from the Persian monarch, spending a huge sum of it on weapons with which he would provide the Thebans. Soon enough, the Greeks were attacking the Macedonian settlements, and it wouldn't be long until word of this revolt reached the young king.

Once Alexander heard the news of this rebellion, he marched straight to Thessaly in order to quell the fighting. Impressively, he had managed to march with his army more than three hundred miles in a period of just two weeks, a feat that would be unheard of even today, despite our modern equipment and far more rigorous military training than in ancient Europe. Not only were the Thebans caught by surprise, but so were the other Greek allies, who promptly abandoned supporting the rebellion. The only real holdouts were Thebes and Athens, as well as Sparta in the beginning, though they pulled out relatively quickly as well.

Alexander would go on to besiege Thebes, but before he would do so, he tried negotiating peace, requiring the delivery of the rebel leaders. Thebes refused, offering demands of its own, and thus, war was inevitable. The siege was relatively difficult, but at one crucial moment, Alexander's general Perdiccas broke through the gates and entered the city. Not long after, the Macedonians claimed victory.

Alexander dealt with the Thebans ruthlessly. He ordered that all of the men of the city be executed and the women and children thrown into slavery. Next, his troops burned the city to the ground, leaving only a few key locations intact, including the house of the poet Pindar. Interestingly, Alexander would spare Athens and Demosthenes; even though he was a bitter adversary to the young prince, he would not die during Alexander's reign. However, Alexander didn't really need to punish Athens. The destruction of Thebes was enough of an indicator to the Greeks that the new king was not to be taken lightly and that any subordination would end in a disaster. Of course, there might have been practical reasons for Alexander keeping Athens unscathed. After all, even during its worst periods of existence, the city-state had one of the best, most active fleets in the Mediterranean, and if he were to crush the Persians, Alexander needed a navy.

Chapter 3 – Alexander's Conquests: Asia Minor, Syria, Egypt, Babylon, Persia, and India

Having crushed the united efforts of Thebes and Athens a mere two weeks after doing the same to the Illyrian and Thracian tribes, Alexander had more than proven himself capable of ruling Macedon and being a hegemon of the League of Corinth. It certainly helped that the young king had such powerful military veterans who used to be in his father's service, such as Cleitus the Black, Parmenion, and Antipater, who came with experience and at least a passing loyalty to the Argead dynasty. However, Alexander also had his own childhood friends and loyal compatriots to serve him, including the ones Philip had exiled because of the Pixodarus incident.

With the Greeks consolidated and the Balkans under relative peace, Alexander was ready to face the Persians. The stage had been long set for this showdown, all the way back to when Philip was in charge, and it was only a matter of time before the new Macedonian king took up the spear and marched toward Asia Minor. He gathered a massive army, composed mostly of Macedonians, and left for the Hellespont in 334, leaving Antipater as the regent of Macedon in his absence. Alexander's conquest had officially begun.

Asia Minor

The Battle of the Granicus River

As stated earlier, Alexander had a navy at his disposal and an experienced one at that. However, it's interesting to note that he didn't engage in any naval battles with the Persians but instead went on to take a different route of defeating them, that of crushing all coastal cities that were the centers of the Persian navy. This was, by far, the more difficult route to take since it would effectively leave Alexander surrounded from both land and sea, and had he used the Athenian navy, the conquest might have gone even smoother than it did. Of course, there might have been a very good reason behind him not using the Athenians. The vast majority of his army, which counted well over seventy thousand troops, was comprised of Upper and Lower Macedonian soldiers and generals, with the Greeks barely participating. Considering he had just spent the better part of 335 killing and conquering the Greeks, it's safe to say that there was a huge level of distrust and distaste for the young king by the non-Macedonian factions. One wrong move, and the young monarch could have had a full-blown rebellion within his ranks. Furthermore, Asia Minor was full of Greek mercenaries, and they often fought for the Persians. More precisely, they fought for Persian wages. As stated earlier, the Persian kings were some of the richest, if not outright *the* richest people at the time. According to early historical accounts, Alexander's troops supposedly plundered 180,000 silver talents at Persepolis alone, while Darius fled with 8,000. If we were to combine those two and convert the sum into modern currency units, that would give the Persian King of Kings a wealth of, at the very least, $3.9 billion. Taking the size of the Achaemenid Empire into consideration, as well as the fact that there were several cities as big as Persepolis with just as much loot, it's safe to say that Darius III would be at least within the top thirty richest people of 2021 had he been alive today.

Indeed, Darius had the money to hire mercenaries, and the Greeks of Asia Minor felt no strong fealty to either their Macedonian or Greek counterparts. For that reason, Alexander was careful to make his army as homogenous as possible before advancing against the Persians. And his first taste of battle on non-European soil would come swiftly once he crossed the Hellespont and dramatically announced his conquest of Asia by piercing his spear into the soil. Interestingly enough, this would be the first and last time he crossed from Europe into Asia, as well as the last time he would ever set foot on Macedonian soil.

The first test of Alexander's military prowess came at the Granicus River (the modern-day Biga River in Turkey), a rather small body of water with some depth. It was prior to this battle that Parmenion advised Alexander to cross the river upstream and wait for the next day before attacking. However, Alexander responded that a delay would give confidence to the Persians and that the Hellespont would surely blush in shame if the Macedonian king were to hesitate before crossing such a small river in his first battle. Therefore, he went straight on the attack, catching the encamped Persians completely off-guard.

Alexander's task was not easy. The forces of Darius III numbered at around thirty thousand, and that number even included a large group of Greek mercenaries, led by a Rhodian Greek general called Memnon. Memnon's own story is just as fascinating as Alexander's; as a Greek from Rhodes, he was not a favorite of the Persians who often employed his services, but as a mercenary, he had even less love from the mainland Greeks, who would also work with him on several occasions in an effort to overthrow Alexander. Despite all of these setbacks, however, Memnon would prove to be both the best defender that the Persian Empire ever had and the only man who came dangerously close to thwarting Alexander and who, had he lived longer, might have even killed the young conqueror. In short, the army Alexander was facing, though not homogenous in terms of nationality, was comprised of seasoned warriors who had the home-field advantage. The young ruler had to get creative in order to defeat them, and the Battle of the Granicus would show just how creative he could be.

During the fighting, Alexander would use clever feint tactics in order to break through the enemy lines. He himself was close to being killed by Spithrodates, a military commander and a satrap of Lydia, who approached the young Macedonian from behind. Luckily, Cleitus the Black would prevent his master's untimely death by cutting off Spithrodates's arm, and the satrap died soon after.

The battle ended with a decisive Macedonian victory, with Persian losses at some four thousand soldiers to death and an additional two thousand to slavery. Memnon of Rhodes would survive the Battle of the Granicus River in one piece, but his fellow Greek mercenaries were not as fortunate. Namely, due to being traitors to the Greek cause and siding with the Persians (an act that no Greek state, no matter how bigoted toward the Persians, was really innocent of, especially during the reign of the Argeads), they had to be punished, and Alexander was just as ruthless as he tended to be in these situations. He would order the deaths of some nine thousand Greek mercenaries from Asia Minor, and out of the remaining nine thousand, eight thousand were sent to Macedon as slaves.

Amusingly, Alexander had also sent three hundred suits of Persian armor to Athens, with the instruction that they be hung in the Parthenon as a votive offering to Athena. He also ordered an inscription be fixed over them that stated, "Alexander, son of Philip, and the Greeks, except of Lacedaemonians, present this offering of the spoils taken from the barbarians who live in Asia"; this move was an obvious and effective way of humiliating the Spartans who had refused to join the League of Corinth and, consequently, refused to provide any troops for Alexander's conquest. The Spartans would come to blows with the Macedonians again, though not directly against Alexander himself but rather Antipater, who would defeat the Spartans while they were laying siege to Megalopolis in 331.

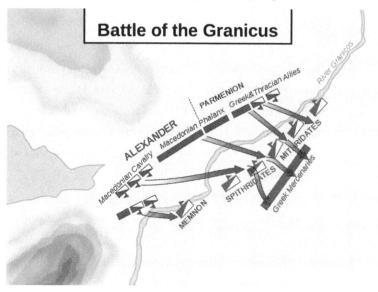

The Battle of the Granicus River, 334 BCE

The Siege of Miletus

Miletus was a prominent Greek city in Asia Minor that had been under Persian occupation for some time during the years Alexander was active. As a coastal city on the eastern shore of what is now modern-day Turkey, Miletus was an important port for the Persian navy, one that Alexander had to crush. Thus, after defeating the Persians at the Granicus River, Alexander continued southeast and reached the city relatively quickly. As soon as he did, he started laying siege, and though it would be a long and difficult battle, Alexander would still come out on top. The biggest problem with this siege was the possible presence of the Persian navy, an issue that Philotas, Parmenion's son, managed to settle during the conflict. Parmenion's other son, Nicanor, would be the one to take control of Miletus in Alexander's name.

The Siege of Halicarnassus and the Gordian Knot

Though Alexander had won Miletus, he was still far from completely routing the Persian navy. The troops moved farther south, reaching the famed city of Halicarnassus, whose ruins lie near the modern Turkish city of Bodrum.

Halicarnassus was an ancient city-state that was technically still ruled by a king despite being both Greek (in nationality as well as culture) and a willing Persian vassal. Thanks to its coastal position and its size, Halicarnassus was the perfect fort for anyone to take refuge in, and Alexander's opponents (including Memnon and a Persian satrap named Orontobates) knew that quite well.

It would be several strokes of luck that managed to save Alexander from losing at Halicarnassus. The first and most obvious would be his meeting the dethroned queen, Ada of Caria. Ada had actually been removed from the throne of Halicarnassus by her younger brother, Pixodarus, and after his death, the city went to Orontobates by means of an official decision by King Darius. With Alexander fighting to wrestle control of Halicarnassus from the clutches of his enemies, he and Ada formed a bit of a friendship, with the senior queen even adopting Alexander and proclaiming that her kingdom should be his by inheritance if she dies.

The battle was not really supposed to happen; it was at best a siege of a castle, but due to the craftiness of Memnon, the Greek mercenaries and the Macedonians fought valiantly against each other. Memnon was clearly winning here, having deployed his catapults and keeping the young king at bay. But it wouldn't be long until Alexander's infantry broke through the city walls and surprised the Persians. Naturally, Memnon was not one to give up something easily; when he spotted that his side was losing, he set fire to Halicarnassus, which destroyed most of the city. Memnon himself retreated to fight another day, while Alexander was left with the scorching remains of the city he had just conquered. In the long term, this victory gave Alexander a massive advantage over his enemies, and his subsequent battles would end in significantly easier victories. But in the short term, it very much looked like a Pyrrhic victory, with both sides losing huge numbers of soldiers and the city itself lying in ruins.

For the most part, the rest of Alexander's campaign in Asia Minor held no significant victories, considering that there was no major port from the plain of Pamphylia. As a result, Alexander moved inward to the Pisidian city of Termessos. Though the city was indeed humbled by Alexander, he did not conquer or storm it. Moving swiftly onward, Alexander would reach Gordium, a city-state well known for its convoluted knot that was notoriously difficult to untangle. Alexander managed to do it, but the exact details of what happened are a bit of romantic legend, at best.

Syria and the Levant

The Battle of Issus

After his string of successes, Alexander moved south to a region called Cilicia (now a part of southern Anatolia) in 333, though not entirely for conquest purposes. Namely, having heard of all the defeats his kinsmen had suffered, King Darius III took command of the army himself and marched in an attempt to crush Alexander. The two rulers would meet in battle near the mouth of the Pinarus River at a town called Issus. The ensuing battle would be one of the most important military outings of Alexander's career.

The area around Issus was originally held by Parmenion, but Darius's army made short work of the city, subjugating it and torturing and mutilating all of the people that Alexander had left behind. In addition, the Persians managed to cut the Macedonians' main supply line, prompting Alexander to act.

The ensuing battle was not easy. At first, Darius's forces pushed Alexander's army back, but Alexander's ingenuity once again came to the forefront; alongside his bodyguards, he would punch a hole through the Persian line and managed to disperse them. Darius had to flee the battle, leaving behind corpses of both Persians and the Greek mercenaries he had hired. Some of the same mercenaries would later agree to help Spartan King Agis III in an uprising against Macedon a few years later. One direct result of Darius fleeing is the fact that he had left most of his family behind at the mercy of Alexander, including his mother Sisygambis, his wife Stateira I, and his daughters, Stateira II and Drypetis. Interestingly, Alexander didn't have them executed (though he never shied away from brutally punishing everyone) and treated them with the utmost respect. He would even go on to marry Stateira II.

The famous Alexander Mosaic from the House of the Faun in Pompeii, circa 100 BCE, supposedly depicting either the Battle of Issus or the Battle of Gaugamela; King Darius III is center-right and Alexander center-left riding Bucephalas, obscured by the damage"

The Siege of Tyre

After taking Issus, Alexander moved farther south, capturing several key areas in ancient Syria and the Middle East, such as the cities of Byblos, Arwad, and Sidon. The last real challenge on the coast was the ancient city of Tyre, a coastal settlement of around forty thousand people whose territory also encompassed a fortified island with famously impenetrable walls. The city itself was not inhabited by Persians but Phoenicians, a seafaring people whose successors would go on to form Carthage in North Africa.

Alexander did not initially want to besiege Tyre. Instead, when he arrived in early 332, he wanted to make a votive offering to Heracles in the city's temple to the god Melqart, whom he saw as merely a different representation of the Greek hero. However, the Tyrians made it perfectly clear that no Persian or Macedonian would set foot in the temple. Alexander tried negotiating again, but the envoys he sent to Tyre were brutally murdered and thrown off the city walls into the sea. Enraged, Alexander ordered a siege, and the ensuing six months would prove to be some of the most grueling for both the Macedonians and the Tyrians.

Initially, Alexander saw little success. He built a massive causeway to the island, considering he had no standing fleet in the beginning, and had his soldiers use two massive siege towers to scale the city walls. However, the Tyrians managed to stave off the attack by burning the siege towers through the use of an old ship that they filled with combustible materials. This was a major setback for Alexander, and had he not conquered most of the Asia Minor and Levantine coast, it might have been his greatest defeat.

As was customary for the past few years, Alexander had no navy but rather did all of his conquering "on foot," crushing or besieging all Persian-held port cities that housed huge harbors and had entry points for fleets of ships. Of course, it was clear from his initial advances (and their failures) that he would not take Tyre by way of land. He would definitely need a navy, and if this had been the Alexander from the start of his Asia Minor campaign, he would have more than likely lost right there. However, this was Alexander with a huge chunk of the Middle East under his sword. As such, he had access to several important cities with fleets of their own. But more importantly, the Cypriot king at the time had heard of Alexander's string of victories and wanted to join him, sending over 120 of his own galleys. More than twenty additional ships came from Ionia, a Greek city-state based in modern-day Anatolia in Turkey. Combined with the ships he had already commanded from the conquered cities, Alexander's fleet now numbered well over two hundred ships, which was more than enough to surround Tyre and breathe new energy into the siege.

Of course, the Tyrians did not make it easy for Alexander. They continued to fight tooth and nail for their city, and it would appear that it was a sheer stroke of luck that Alexander would win the fight. Namely, the Tyrian soldiers had paid attention to Alexander's habits during the battlefield, noting when he went to eat and rest during the day. Using that specific timeframe, they initiated a surprise attack on the Macedonians, but thanks to the swift arrival of backup soldiers, including Alexander himself, the attack was thwarted. Throughout the latter part of the siege, Alexander's army was chipping away at the walls with battering rams until an opening was finally made. With ferocity, the Macedonians forced their way into the city and took it with little effort.

Alexander was extremely vengeful toward the Tyrians. Most of the men were slain, with some two thousand of them crucified on the beach in front of the city. Women and children were largely sold into slavery. The only people who were spared were those who took refuge in the temple of Melqart, including the Tyrian king, Azemilcus. Alexander now controlled nearly the entire coastal area of the Middle East, save for one strip of land that connected Asia and Africa. With Tyre now under his belt, the young king set about to conquer that area as well, providing his new empire an expansion into a third continent.

Egypt

The Siege of Gaza and the Surrender of Egypt

Before Alexander could reach Gaza, several cities that were in the way quickly surrendered to him. By this point, he had already built up a reputation of a conqueror, and as was the case with the areas leading up to Tyre, certain cities simply did not want to take that risk and chose vassalage instead. This, of course, provided Alexander with more prestige and elevated his achievements further. But more importantly, it gave him new supplies of slaves, soldiers, and goods. His next move was to march toward Egypt and take control of it, but one key site stood in his way—Gaza.

Gaza was a fort located on an eminence on the edge of a desert. Even back then, the region had been extremely volatile, but the position of the fortress and the sweeping view of the area it provided made it perfect for controlling the region. More importantly, it had been strategically placed in such a position as to overlook major routes to and from Egypt. In other words, if Alexander wanted to conquer the land of the pharaohs of old, he had to go through Gaza first.

At the time, the commander of the fortress was a Darius loyalist and a eunuch called Batis. Having heard of Alexander's exploits, he correctly assumed that the young Macedonian king (now dangerously close to bearing a different, more prestigious title) would be going for Gaza once he finished besieging Tyre, so he prudently prepared his fortress to withstand a long siege. Batis was determined to resist Alexander to the bitter end, a commendable feat knowing that his adversary had taken most of coastal Persia and had even defeated the King of Kings in open battle (and, to make matters worse, held the king's family as prisoners).

Alexander arrived at Gaza near the end of 332 and stationed his troops alongside the southern walls of the fortress, deeming them to be the weakest. He then ordered his engineers to build massive mounds around the city, which they were hesitant about, maintaining that they would be impossible to build as quickly as Alexander needed them due to the nature of Gaza's terrain. Nevertheless, the mounds were erected all around the fort, mostly as a result of one Gazan sortie that left some of Alexander's builders murdered and the equipment for mound-building damaged.

At a certain point, Alexander would receive the best help possible. Siege equipment from the newly conquered Tyre arrived, and Alexander used it on the mounds in order to gain access to Gaza's inner walls. After three unsuccessful attempts, the Macedonians finally entered the city, where they were met by stiff Gazan resistance. During the fighting, Alexander would receive a serious wound on his shoulder.

Batis, to his credit, refused to surrender to Alexander, even when the battle was clearly over in the young Macedonian king's favor. Usually, Alexander would show leniency toward a worthy opponent, provided he surrendered and accepted Alexander as his master. Instead of doing that, Batis simply acted arrogantly and annoyed Alexander to the point of the young conqueror punishing the eunuch in the worst way imaginable. Mirroring Achilles's defeating of Hector, Alexander had the Gazan commander bound to a horse and ordered that the animal should drag his lifeless body in front of everyone.

However, infinitely more interesting than his sieges was Alexander's relatively uneventful conquest of Egypt. When he arrived with his troops, the local satrap immediately surrendered to the young king, making this possibly the most significant of Alexander's conquests that went off without a single drop of blood shed. Alexander would spend the winter in Egypt, carefully organizing the region and appointing his men to some of the key positions, most notably Cleomenes as the treasurer of both Upper and Lower Egypt. As a treasurer, Cleomenes would amass a huge amount of wealth, which Ptolemy acquired after the treasurer's death. Consequently, Ptolemy was in Egypt with Alexander as well, though he would only come to prominence in this region after the young conqueror had been long dead.

While he was in Egypt, Alexander expressed the desire to visit the famed oracle to the god Amon, located in the Siwa Oasis in modern-day Libya. Reportedly, Alexander wanted to seek advice from both Zeus and Heracles, equating Zeus to Amon (he would not be the first

Macedonian or even the first Hellenic person to do so). After consulting the oracle, he claimed to be the son of Zeus-Ammon, in an odd blend of the two deities. Moreover, on Alexander's official coinage, he would be depicted with the Horns of Ammon, an old symbol of the Egyptian deity. The exact reasons he adopted this custom and claimed to be the son of an Egyptian god are still a matter of debate among historians. He might have done so due to a genuine religious awakening, or he might have just used the religion of the locals to further legitimize his position as the main figurehead of Egypt. If that were the case, it worked like a charm, as he was proclaimed pharaoh during his stay there, and his name even appears in ancient hieroglyphs.

One habit that Alexander had inherited from his father was a penchant for forming cities in areas he had conquered. And as it tends to be the case, he would unimaginatively name those cities after himself. That's why there were more than a dozen Alexandrias all over the ancient world. However, when we mention Alexandria today, one particular city comes to mind, that built in Egypt.

There were several reasons behind Alexander founding the city where he did. First of all, it was close to the Nile Delta, a fertile area where inland water transport was plentiful. Next, the area offered sheltered deep-water anchorage. Furthermore, the delta provided more than enough fresh water for a large town. Finally, the location was conveniently placed west from Asia Minor, with a direct open route to the Aegean Sea. In other words, it provided Alexander with an excellent method of patrolling the waters and providing backup in case some foreign invader decided to attack the Asia Minor coastal cities or one of the many islands now under Macedonian control.

Alexandria would not be a huge city during Alexander's lifetime. However, it would soon grow to be a proper capital to the Egyptians, as well as the center for future Macedonian rulers of the land belonging to the Ptolemaic dynasty. Not only would it be the home of the well-known lighthouse located on the island of Pharos (one of the

Seven Wonders of the Ancient World), but it would also house one of the biggest, best-equipped libraries and largest repositories of knowledge in the ancient past, the famous Library of Alexandria.

Unlike Tyre, Issus, and other ancient cities that Alexander besieged, Egypt did not see the Macedonian ruler as an enemy. In fact, he was treated as a hero and a liberator from the yoke of the Persians. Of course, Alexander would continue to loosen that yoke further in the coming years, but before he did, he repaid Egyptian loyalty with careful planning, massive rebuilding plans, and a newfound interest in their divine matters. With Egypt under his belt, Alexander now controlled all of the eastern Mediterranean, a fact not lost on the people around him. And while it is true that he had succeeded in this massive undertaking through sheer genius and resilience during the sieges of the coastal cities, there were two other factors that helped him along the way. Firstly, Memnon, his most powerful adversary, had died in 333 during the siege of Mytilene, the ancient capital of the island of Lesbos. Secondly, after the Battle of Issus, Persian refugees tried to reach the Persian fleet in the Aegean Sea for support, but they were repelled by the Greater Phrygian commander of Alexander's, a man named Antigonus One-Eyed, who had managed to defeat them on three separate occasions. Both of these events left the Levant largely free for the taking, and though Alexander did struggle with besieging certain areas after Antigonus's victories and the death of Memnon, he would have done infinitely worse had Memnon not lost his life mid-siege.

Assyria and Babylon

The Battle of Gaugamela

After his exploits in Egypt, Alexander left for Tyre once again, aiming to move eastward toward Babylon. In order to reach it, he would have to cross both the Euphrates and Tigris Rivers, the famed bodies of water from which Mesopotamia got its name. In crossing the Euphrates, Alexander would encounter one of Darius III's commanders, Mazaeus, and he would proceed to defeat his army and force him to flee. Crossing the Tigris was the more difficult task, considering the depth of the river and its strong currents, but Alexander nevertheless managed to do it. He would face further difficulties since Mazaeus had employed scorched earth tactics in retreating, i.e., he burned all the grain and destroyed all of the possible sources of supplies that Alexander might come across. Of course, Alexander's troops prevailed, and they would once again defeat a minor contingent of the Persian army after the Tigris crossing and another one after a lunar eclipse took place, estimated to be on October 1st, 331. The prisoners taken from this minor contingent would let Alexander know that King Darius had an encampment nearby, at the wide-open field called Gaugamela (the name of the field derives from the Semitic word *gammalu*, meaning "dromedary" or what we would later call "Arabian camel"; the field was close to a small hill that reminded the Persians of a dromedary's hump).

The ensuing Battle of Gaugamela would prove to be one of the most important conflicts in ancient history, not just because of its sheer scale (in total, there might have been as many as 200,000 troops involved), but because of its consequences and reverberations in the decades to come. It would signal the end of an ancient empire and the forging of a new one, but more importantly, it would establish Hellenistic culture as the dominant force in the region for centuries. Furthermore, it would confirm, without a shadow of a doubt, that Alexander was the undisputed power in the region and that Macedon was a force to be reckoned with.

Of course, there were attempts to prevent the battle from even taking place. According to ancient historians, Darius and Alexander tried to broker a treaty at least three times. Darius's third attempt at negotiations saw him offering thirty thousand talents and his daughter's hand in marriage to Alexander, in addition to the young king keeping the territories he had already conquered. Alexander refused the offer, claiming that the empire was rightfully his already.

This was not a good sign for Darius; after having lost every single coastal city to Alexander and, more importantly, having lost the Battle of Issus against the young king personally, he was no longer a king that the people of the Achaemenid Empire could rely on. And while he still commanded a huge force and had enough wealth to buy his way out of every situation, he was no longer the powerful monarch a Persian subject had come to expect. Moreover, plenty of territories simply surrendered to Alexander without as much as lifting a sword to defend themselves and not just because of the Macedonian king's prowess. They were, in fact, using the opportunity of a weakened empire to reclaim some shred of sovereignty or to simply free themselves from the Persians, even at the expense of serving Macedon.

Darius, of course, knew all of that, so his victory at Gaugamela had to be decisive. He gathered an army that might have numbered as many as 120,000 troops, including 10,000 Persian Immortals (the king's royal guard and a form of a standing army), some 8,000 Greek mercenaries, 200 scythed chariots (battle vehicles with scythes sticking out of the wheels), and 15 war elephants. Of course, for such a massive army, Darius needed the best possible terrain, and the field of Gaugamela served precisely that purpose. Aside from the aforementioned hill, there were no major geographical obstacles there, meaning Darius could spread his army out as much as he needed to and give them room to maneuver. He also ordered his army to flatten the terrain further in preparation for the battle. Furthermore, there were no major bodies of water nearby. Considering the dry and hot autumn climate, this factor would play to his home-field advantage since most Macedonians were not accustomed to the Mesopotamian weather, and the lack of water would be a major factor in maintaining morale. Finally, Gaugamela was nowhere near as narrow as Issus, a major issue that contributed to Darius losing to Alexander several years before.

Alexander's army was much smaller in scale but equally impressive. The most elite forces would belong to the Companions, or *hetairoi*, also known as the Companion Cavalry, a group of largely Macedonian nobles who also served as the commanders of the troops. The seven most prominent men out of the Companion Cavalry would form the so-called *somatophylakes*, or the personal bodyguards of the king. In addition, there were the Foot Companions (*pezhetairoi*) or the light infantry, and the Shield Bearers (*hypaspistai*), light infantrymen with small shields and long pole weapons who protected the flanks. Estimates suggest that Alexander's army could have numbered anywhere up to fifty thousand troops.

Both armies were commanded by skilled warriors, and Alexander's troops, in particular, were led by some of his most prominent friends and later successors to the empire. Hephaestion and Parmenion were there, with the latter being in direct command of the left flank of the army. In addition, Craterus, Nearchus, Cleitus the Black, Antigonus the One-Eyed, Ptolemy Soter, Perdiccas, and Seleucus Nicator, among others, found themselves in the heat of battle. The Persian side also had a few notable names commanding the troops, with Mazaeus being right there next to the king, as well as Bessus, a relative of the king who would play a far more prominent role after the battle. The two men commanded the right and the left flank, respectively, with Darius, as was custom, being in the middle. Interestingly, both armies were quite diverse, containing mercenaries from various tribes (sometimes, those mercenaries would be kinsmen; both Darius and Alexander had Greek hired swords from Asia Minor) who excelled in different areas, be they archers, infantry, or carriage riders.

The battle started with Alexander's infantry marching at the center of Darius's line in a typical Macedonian phalanx formation, where the heavy-armed troopers with spears or similar pole weapons would advance in close proximity to each other with their shields up, forming an almost impenetrable rectangle. Darius responded by sending a portion of his troops to the left to tackle Parmenion's men. It was during this time that Alexander employed a unique and extremely risky strategy of moving to the extreme right and drawing the Persian troops away, forcing them to leave a gap in the center where Darius would be exposed. The plan worked since Darius had to send some forces after the young king. Darius's Scythian cavalry was the one to engage Alexander in battle, and the fighting was grueling, especially considering the fact that the Macedonian troops were outnumbered. However, they continued to push onward, slowly thinning out the numbers of the Persian army at the right flank. In the meantime, Darius kept dispensing more and more troops to the flanks, playing right into Alexander's hands. Not even the chariots managed to do any harm, as they were picked off by Macedonian javelins and the armed forces surrounding them.

With the flanks fighting and the center facing off against the phalanx, Alexander saw a chance, so he disengaged slowly from his Companion Cavalry and mustered all of the available troops around him, forming a massive wedge with him leading the charge. This force struck at the Persian center from the right, and with the Persians in the center fighting the phalanxes, they were unable to push back immediately. Alexander and his troops annihilated most of the Persian Immortal elites and the Greek mercenaries stationed nearby, inching dangerously close to Darius himself. Sources differ at this point, with some historians claiming that the King of King's army started abandoning him, while others claim that was not the case. The outcome was in effect the same—Darius fled the battlefield with a huge portion of his troops following him.

However, the battle was far from over. Parmenion's flank was being overwhelmed by the Persians, so Alexander turned back to help his general, missing the chance of killing Darius in the process. A huge portion of the Persian army, which contained Indian and Parthian infantry, broke through the Macedonian center and went straight for their camp, partially to loot but also to liberate the queen mother, Sisygambis. However, considering how kindly Alexander had treated her and her family up to that point, Sisygambis refused to leave the camp. In the meantime, the rear guard of the Macedonian army turned back and encircled the Persian looters. By far the most intense stage of the battle took place then, with the massive Persian army trying to break through to escape and the Macedonians trying to hold them off. Many of Alexander's generals, including Hephaestion, were injured during the fighting. Mazaeus was in charge of this contingent, and as soon as the Macedonians turned the tide of the war, he decided to retreat, as did Darius and Bessus before him. It was a decisive victory for Alexander and possibly the biggest defeat of the Persians in history.

Darius did not sit still after this defeat, however. After retreating, with Bessus not far behind, the King of Kings tried desperately to get the satraps to join him in defending what little remained of the empire. And while some men did still swear fealty to him, others deserted to Alexander, including Mazaeus. In fact, it would be Mazaeus who would open the doors of Babylon and allow Alexander to enter, resulting in the satrap's pardon and consequent appointment of the Babylonian satrapy.

Clay cuneiform astronomical diary describing Alexander's victory at Gaugamela and his triumphant entry into Babylon, 331-330 BCE, British Museum[vii]

Persia

The Battle of the Persian Gate

Now a fully recognized conqueror, Alexander would go on to take city after city the more eastward he went. Babylon and Susa, two of the Persian capitals, gave up without a fight, and as such, they were left relatively unharmed by Alexander. Furthermore, their treasuries replenished his budget and gave his troops further cause for conquest. However, there was still one capital that he had to subdue for his conquest to be complete (notwithstanding the fact that he still had to eliminate Darius), and that would be the famed ancient city of Persepolis.

Before reaching the city, which, in 330, was governed by the satrap Ariobarzanes, Alexander split his army into two halves, with Parmenion heading one contingent along the Persian Royal Road and the young king himself leading the other contingent through the treacherous mountain range that stood between Susa and Persepolis. The king of Macedon had to face the Uxian tribesmen that dwelled in this mountain range. A victory here would leave nothing between the Macedonians and Ariobarzanes's city, and indeed, Alexander did subdue the Uxians and proceeded to march onward. Ariobarzanes knew that there was only one way he could prevent Alexander from advancing, and that was by taking hold of a narrow mountain pass called the Persian Gate. It would be here that Ariobarzanes would wait with a small number of troops (around two thousand, at most) and ambush the Macedonian army, which was nearly five times the size of what the satrap had commanded.

Alexander was not ready for this ambush, and his huge army could not easily maneuver the narrow mountain pass, especially during the winter months. His troops were attacked from above with boulders and from below by archers, and Alexander had to retreat, leaving a huge number of dead soldiers behind, a shameful act considering how much emphasis Macedonians placed on burying their dead.

Ariobarzanes held the Persian Gate for a month, with Alexander continuously advancing until he managed to encircle the Persians in a pincer attack, largely thanks to Philotas, Parmenion's son. Though caught by surprise, the Persians made this battle their last stand, fighting tooth and nail against the Macedonians. Some reports suggest that they even fought barehanded, with Ariobarzanes's own sister Youtab joining the fray. The satrap himself was trapped, but he would not surrender, instead choosing to charge at the Macedonians head-on. At some point, however, his troops had to flee, and whether he was among them or not is still a matter of debate among scholars. The troops reached Persepolis but were denied entry and were subsequently killed at the city walls by the incoming Macedonian troops.

The Battle of the Persian Gate would prove to be one of the single most difficult battles of Alexander's career. His victory came at a massive cost, considering how many of his men needlessly died trying to wedge themselves through the narrow pass. Moreover, there was also a symbolic and somewhat ironic side to this battle. Namely, even at the time, historians compared Ariobarzanes's last stand to that of Leonidas at the Battle of Thermopylae; both battles took place in a narrow pass, both defending armies were few in number yet resilient to the end, and both invading armies would prevail but with heavy losses. The ironic part was that in Thermopylae, the Persians were the invaders. This last stand was, in effect, a sort of moral vengeance against the Greeks (or, in this case, Macedonians, which made little difference to an average Persian), and it undoubtedly made Ariobarzanes a legend, rightfully earning him the moniker Ariobarzanes the Brave.

Persepolis, like Susa and Babylon, would open its gates to Alexander. However, despite initially treating the city relatively well, save for the mandatory looting, roughly four months after his entry within its walls, Alexander ordered the looting and the burning of the city, as well as the execution of all men and the rape and enslavement of women. The reasons behind this order are still unclear to historians, but some suggest he might have done so as a final act of vengeance against the Persians.

In March 330, after this massive crushing of the Persians and the ruination of Persepolis, Alexander would set off to finally locate and kill Darius. However, he was apparently shocked to find out about the fate of the King of Kings. In 330, Bessus had Darius III imprisoned while they were all fleeing to Bactria. Not long after, Bessus had Darius killed, and not long after that, he proclaimed himself King of Kings and took the name Artaxerxes V. Technically, he would have been a legitimate ruler considering his lineage, but neither ancient nor modern historians see him as a legitimate ruler, and neither did Alexander. Reportedly, after learning about Darius's death, the Macedonian king was stricken with grief. He supposedly saw Darius as a noble adversary, and learning that he had died in such an ignoble way (betrayed by a former general, chained, and stabbed to death by multiple people while in chains) enraged him to the point of wanting Bessus's head. Of course, we should keep in mind that the act of a king feeling sorrow for his opponent's death was a bit of a cliché back in the day, one that was more propaganda than truth and one that came especially handy when consolidating the rival's people. Indeed, Alexander would have Darius buried in Persepolis with the highest honors around the same time he was legally proclaimed King of Kings. In addition, he might have wanted Bessus's head for simply depriving him of the chance to take Darius's life himself.

Bessus would be betrayed by his fellow countrymen to the Macedonians, and Ptolemy threw the usurper king in chains and dragged him in front of Alexander for questioning. Bessus claimed that he saw Darius as unfit for kingship, which prompted him to claim the title himself, and that he wasn't the only noble who wanted Darius deposed. Alexander was not satisfied with this response, which resulted in Bessus being whipped at the city of Bactra (modern-day Balkh), then taken to have his ears and nose lopped off, and finally to be executed, most likely in Ecbatana, another ancient city in Media.

The Indian Campaign

The Battle of the Hydaspes

Persia was now Alexander's. He was the undisputed ruler, and he had control of the major Persian cities, the vast Persian navy, and the Royal Road. At this point, it was pretty clear that any pretense of a Pan-Hellenic alliance was gone and that Alexander was now acting as any conqueror would—greedy for more territories and recognition. The vast majority of his army now comprised of the local people groups, despite the Macedonians still being at the top of the proverbial food chain. Naturally, Alexander wanted his empire to encompass the same territory Persia had during its heyday, and according to contemporary sources, it had expanded well into the territory beyond the Indus River. Additional eastern conquests were inevitable, and the period between 327 and 325 would mark Alexander's famed Indian campaign.

However, before he could reach India, he had to settle a few things in Asia Minor. In 329, he besieged the extremely fortified city of Cyropolis, located in ancient Sogdiana (modern-day Tajikistan). He took it but sustained massive wounds from the battle. Next, he had to face the Saka nomadic warriors beyond the Jaxartes River, managing to subdue them in battle in late 329. He ended up releasing their prisoners without ransom, a tactic that was incredibly prudent considering that the Saka did not attack him further after their defeat. The most important event before the Indian campaign, however, had to be the Siege of the Sogdian Rock in 327.

Located north of Bactria in ancient Sogdiana, near modern-day Samarkand in Uzbekistan, the Sogdian Rock was a supposedly impenetrable fortress, and due to its reputation, the people had refused to surrender to Alexander. However, through the use of clever psychological warfare, he managed to convince them otherwise, and the story of said conquest has become one of many legends revolving around the Macedonian king. But the siege itself isn't particularly important for the future course of events. Or rather, it was important in terms of strategic positioning and Alexander's future military exploits but not as important as a different event that took place at the Rock.

During the aftermath of Gaugamela, sometime around 329, the still-alive Bessus retreated to Sogdiana with his servants, one of whom was a minor noble called Oxyartes. After the death of Bessus and having learned of Alexander's advances, Oxyartes placed his wife and his daughters in the Sogdian Rock, deeming it to be the safest place for them. Two years later, Alexander would take the Rock, though he would treat the prisoners with respect, especially women. One of the women he supposedly fell instantly in love with was Oxyartes's daughter, Roxane. In fact, Alexander was so smitten by her that he announced he would marry her, a necessary step in providing an heir to his empire. Oxyartes supposedly hurried to the Rock when he heard of the news, promising to pledge his loyalty to the Macedonian King of Kings and to officially offer his daughter's hand in marriage. The ceremony would take place after Alexander took another impenetrable fortress, the Rock of Chorienes, and the siege supposedly took less time than that in Sogdiana due to Oxyartes urging Chorienes to surrender. From there, Alexander would move to Bactra to plan his conquest of India, and it would be in Bactra where he and Roxane got married.

Not long after the wedding, Alexander set out to conquer India, more specifically the Indian territories that were once part of the Achaemenid Empire. His first major campaign, collectively called the Cophen campaign after the namesake river, saw Alexander facing several different Indian clans, the Aspasioi of the Kunar valley (modern Pakistan and Afghanistan), the Guraeans of the Guraeus valley (the valley of the modern-day Panjkora River in Pakistan), and the Assakenoi of the Swat and Buner valleys (both rivers in modern Pakistan). He would claim victory after victory, with one especially brutal siege of the city of Massaga, where the Macedonians committed untold atrocities due to the local Assakenoi not wanting to surrender the Massagan king and serve under Alexander. However, unlike most of his victories in Persia, the ones he gained in India were hard-won and would definitely put both him and his men to the test.

Some of the surviving Assakenoi fled to the fortress of Aornos, and Alexander's advance on the city would be the last siege of his military career. Taking the city was incredibly difficult due to the terrain below and the difficulty of building a mound to bridge the ravine. Somewhat bizarrely, the men of Aornos would repel the Macedonian forces with boulders for three days and celebrate the initial defense with drumbeats, only to completely retreat from the city on the fourth day. Alexander would clear the summit himself, slay a few fugitives along the way, and erect several altars to Athena Nike.

With Aornos taken, Alexander could proceed beyond the Indus River into Punjab. His next target was King Porus of the ancient Paurava kingdom, which lay on the bank of the Hydaspes River (modern-day Jhelum). Porus had refused to submit to Alexander beforehand, and the Macedonian king had to defeat him in order to pursue his goals farther east. In addition, Alexander had allied with the king of Taxila, Taxiles (Ambhi Kumar), who would greatly benefit from Porus's defeat.

Alexander reached the river in May of 326, and his first task was to somehow cross it. Hydaspes, however, was fast and deep, thus completely unfit for anyone to cross. Through a careful strategy of feints, terrain exploration, nighttime advances, reduction of his units' sizes, and appointments of proper battle plans to his main camp under the command of Craterus on the other side of the river, Alexander managed to slip by Porus and cross the river. Before the battle even started, Porus's namesake son lost his life when his expedition, which had been sent by the king, met the Macedonians and was attacked by a flurry of arrows. Porus immediately charged after Alexander, leaving behind a small force to safeguard the bank in case Craterus decided to cross it.

The Indian forces were arranged with the light cavalry and the chariots on the flanks and the infantry in the center, with the war elephants spaced in between. King Porus himself rode an elephant, and each beast was clad in armor and carried a castle-like howdah (mounted carriage) with three soldiers, either archers or javelin throwers. Alexander would focus on the flanks first, devastating the cavalry while leading the charge himself. The Macedonian center infantry had incredible difficulty facing the Indians, though the Indians would end up being caught in a pincer attack thanks to one of Alexander's greatest generals during the Indian campaign,

Parmenion's son-in-law, Coenus. Crushed, the cavalry retreated to the war elephants, whose immense power and force decimated the Macedonian troops. Nevertheless, the soldiers focused on hitting the animals in the eyes or hamstringing their legs, while some aimed for the riders. Riderless elephants would cause a great deal of havoc, trampling on everyone in their sight and fleeing from the battle, leaving the Indians completely exposed to Alexander's forces. Not long after, Craterus would manage to cross the river and provide much-needed help to his king.

Alexander wanted Porus to surrender and sent several messengers to the Pauravan king, all of whom were repelled by his anger (including Taxiles, Porus's bitter rival). The person who finally managed to convince Porus to listen to Alexander's proposal was his friend, Meroes. After demanding water and receiving it, Porus finally agreed to meet the Macedonian monarch, and Alexander himself rode out to see him.

Alexander recognized Porus's spectacular feats in battle, and upon the Indian king's surrender, he was made a subordinate to Macedon and retained his dominion over Paurava. He had lost two sons and a close relative in the battle, as well as most of his chieftains. In addition, Alexander would claim eighty of his elephants from this battle, with an additional seventy provided as an offering to him by the Pauravan reinforcements who came late to the battlefield and promptly surrendered. It had been a hard-fought battle, but Alexander had won.

Coins of Alexander the Great in India, depicting battle elephants, circa 4ᵗʰ century BCE[viii]

Chapter 4 – Alexander's Final Years: Retreat, Wedding at Susa, and Death

Retreat from India

Alexander would found two cities near the Hydaspes River, naming one Nicaea ("victory" in Greek) and Alexandria Bucephalus, named in honor of his horse. A faithful companion throughout his conquest, his horse had died at Hydaspes, possibly of old age (he was pushing thirty), though some authors at the time claim it was due to sustaining fatal injuries on the battlefield. Alexander had the horse buried at the site, and modern historians believe the animal might have been buried near the modern-day town of Jalalpur Sharif in Pakistan.

The troops were due to continue pushing east, beyond the Ganges River, where the Nanda and the Gangaridai empires lay. However, Alexander would not go beyond the Hyphasis River (Beas River in modern-day India) due to his soldiers revolting, demanding to go back home. The Indian campaign had drained them, and the harsh weather and unstable terrain terrified them. In addition, the prospect of crossing a dangerously big Ganges River was unimaginable to them, especially after having to deal with the equally treacherous but significantly smaller Hydaspes. Moreover, the empires they were going to face were far larger and more dangerous than the ones before. After some pleading from his veteran general Coenus, Alexander finally relented, and the armies turned around and went westward, back to Persia. They would reach Susa in 324, but Alexander would lose many men in the process due to constant minor battles, harsh weather, and the dreaded terrain of the Gedrosian desert (in modern Baluchistan).

The Mass Wedding at Susa

Possibly one of the most controversial moments of Alexander's reign was the mass wedding he organized at Susa. The Macedonian King of Kings had already married Roxane several years prior, but Persian customs allowed polygamy, so he selected a few additional wives, including Darius's daughter Stateira II and Artaxerxes III's daughter Parysatis. Drypetis, the sister of Stateira, became Hephaestion's wife, and both Seleucus and Ptolemy married women of Persian nobility. What's more, over ten thousand Macedonians who had been in informal unions with Persian women received legitimization by Alexander, turning their short-lived or long-lived affairs into proper marriages, and each of them received a dowry from the king. The weddings were done according to Persian customs, and Alexander himself wore an outfit that combined Hellenistic and Persian elements.

Alexander's motive for these weddings was that of a union that had to be more than purely political. By marrying Macedonians and Persians, he would bring the two cultures closer together for a more united and homogenous empire. Furthermore, the resulting children would inherit the satrapies, acting as the new elite that combined bloodlines from all people groups. However, there was also a practical side to Alexander's decision to intermarry his subjects. Firstly, all of his wives belonged to the Persian nobility, with two of them, in particular, being from the Achaemenid dynasty. This gave him even more legitimacy among the locals when it came to holding the Persian throne, as he would be continuing in the footsteps of the former Persian rulers. Furthermore, it would keep the Macedonians satisfied, providing them with the highest positions and making them members of nobility almost overnight.

Needless to say, the Macedonian and Greek nobles who were in his army were less than satisfied with this decision. Despite Alexander's conquest taking on a decidedly megalomaniacal turn and the young king's obsession with obtaining huge swathes of territory (and the obsession of his troops in obtaining more spoils of war in the form of loot, grain, and territory), the Hellenistic faction of his army still remembered the original reason behind all of the wars, sieges, and campaigns, that of the Pan-Hellenic union against Persia. As stated earlier, the Macedonians and Greeks agreed on few things, but the one singular issue where they were of one mind was seeing the Persians as barbarians who needed to be dealt with swiftly. So, being a Macedonian nobleman, or even a penniless Macedonian soldier, and learning that all of a sudden, your king and supreme commander has organized a massive wedding with barbarian women as brides, with the express intent to unite the two peoples into one, must have felt like a slap in the face, at the very least. The Macedonians already had to tolerate a lot of changes with their king; not only did he adopt strange new customs of dress and declare himself the successor king of Persian monarchs (from the same dynasty that had been fighting the Greek nations for centuries), but he had also declared himself the son of a foreign god (Zeus-Ammon, as Alexander called him) and had adopted some of the foreign customs that the Hellenistic world saw as abhorrent and beneath them (the best-known example of this being *proskynesis*, or prostrating oneself in front of a ruler and adoring them as a god). And to make matters worse, Alexander's practice of recruiting foreign troops and teaching them Macedonian tactics was equally repulsive. More than thirty thousand soldiers from all over Persia, be they Sogdian, Bactrian, Babylonian, or Levantine, became regulars in Alexander's army, were learning Greek, and had even received commanding positions. An average Macedonian must have seen this as absurd, and even if they were to adore Alexander for his victories and conquests, they surely must have despised him for these acts. One straw that broke the proverbial camel's back was when Alexander, in June of 324, took his soldiers from Babylon to Opis, a northern city on the banks of the Tigris. While there, his Macedonian troops came face to face with a new, young Persian force some thirty thousand strong, and Alexander made an error in calling these youths the "successors" of the Macedonian veterans. Around ten thousand of those veterans were demobilized as no longer fit for service, and naturally, their reaction was to openly rebel. Alexander might have actually anticipated this outcome since his next move was to order them to go back to Macedon, with Craterus in charge of taking them back. Before they moved on, however, Alexander took an oath of unity before both the Macedonian and the Persian soldiers, referring to all of his troops by the Persian honorific of "kinsmen." However, it was clear that there would be no real unity between the Persians and the Hellenes, a sentiment that everyone seemed to agree on.

The Susa weddings engraving, late 19ᵗʰ century[ᵏ]

The Death of Hephaestion

After the mass Susa wedding in 324, Alexander and Hephaestion visited the city of Ecbatana, arriving there in autumn. The sources all state that while there, as a spectator of the local games and festivals, Hephaestion caught a fever and fell ill. The fever apparently lasted for seven days, and evidently, Hephaestion had ignored his doctor's orders at the time, and the reaction came after his excessive eating and drinking. Alexander rushed to be at his friend's side, but he did not make it in time, as Hephaestion was already dead when he arrived.

The death of Hephaestion utterly devastated Alexander. The two men were extremely close, and it's more than likely that they were also lovers for the majority of their formative years. Ancient writers do not expressly call them lovers, and every time Hephaestion is mentioned, he is stated to be nothing more than a loyal friend. However, a clue to their romantic, or at the very least sexual, relationship might be the fact that they were at one point compared to Achilles and Patroclus, who were famously depicted even back in Greco-Roman times as homoerotic. However, homosexual or not, their bond was extremely strong. Hephaestion was at Alexander's side since their common schooling by Aristotle, and ever since the first time Alexander had crossed the Hellespont, the two were nearly inseparable. Not long before, Alexander had also lost his beloved horse Bucephalas, and this loss, coupled with the troubles among his troops and the frequency of new uprisings in Macedon and Persia, crushed Alexander more than any military defeat would.

Hephaestion's body was taken from Ecbatana to Babylon, where Alexander ordered the construction of a huge funeral pyre sixty meters high and consisting of seven ornamented levels. Because of its complexity and extravagance, it was most likely not meant to be burned. In addition to this pyre, Alexander organized expensive funeral games with some three thousand men participating. Throughout the empire, people mourned the fallen Hephaestion, and

Alexander even went so far as to commission some of his subjects to ask the oracle of Siwa (the same one he visited in his spiritual awakening and linkage to Zeus-Ammon) if Hephaestion was allowed to be worshiped as a god. The answer he received was that the fallen man should not be worshiped as a god but rather as a divine hero, which Alexander accepted and ordered his subjects to do. As a final token of Alexander's respect, he ordered that the eternal flame at the temple of Babylon be extinguished, an act that was solely reserved for the death of the King of Kings. In total, more than ten thousand talents were spent on Hephaestion's funeral, a sum that dwarfs the net worth of some of the richest people today.

The Death of Alexander

A year after Hephaestion's death, in June 323, Alexander would fall ill. He was in the midst of some highly intriguing invasion plans, some of which evidently included an invasion of Arabia. However, those plans would never be fulfilled, neither by him nor his successors. In fact, they had an entirely different thing in mind, as we shall see in the following chapters.

Alexander would struggle for a little while after falling ill, finally succumbing to his condition possibly on June 10th of the same year. Scholars today still debate what the cause of his death might have been. Some common theories that involve foul play usually go with the poison route, implicating various individuals as ordering the king's death, including some of his friends and mentors like Antipater and even Aristotle. Others claim that anything from overdrinking to depression over Hephaestion's death might have caused his deteriorating health, which is not outside of the realm of possibility. However, with the symptoms we know of, as described by the most reliable of ancient sources, Alexander most likely died of either malaria or typhoid fever, which was quite common in Babylon and the surrounding cities. Prior to his death, Alexander had been sweating profusely, was often exhausted, had high fever and chills, and might have even had abdominal pain. All of these symptoms point to an infectious disease as the culprit. Moreover, the number of injuries he had sustained throughout his life might have also contributed to his body shutting down. He was prone to injuring himself due to charging head-first into battle, a trait he picked up from his father.

Locating the tomb of Alexander today is impossible. His body was slowly transferred from Babylon to Macedon after he had been embalmed. However, halfway through the transport, his companion and general Ptolemy would claim the body and take it to Memphis in Egypt, where Alexander would be reburied. Not long after, as the sovereign ruler of Egypt, Ptolemy once again transferred Alexander's body to Alexandria, which he had made his capital. Augustus, the first Roman emperor, would visit Alexander's resting place himself and pay his respects. However, as early as the 4th century CE, the whereabouts of the Macedonian king's resting place became unknown. Some speculate that it had been transferred underneath an early Christian church, but that information is far from verified.

Chapter 5 – Alexander, the Man: Physical Appearance, Traits, Beliefs, and Motivations

Physical Appearance of Alexander the Great

There is a wealth of depictions of Alexander the Great dating from antiquity, and while most of them share the same features (indeed, some of the features that would come to be completely associated with Alexander), we still cannot rely on them completely when trying to envisage what the conqueror of Persia looked like. During his life, Alexander appointed two chief artists, a sculptor named Lysippus and a painter named Apelles, to work on his portraits. In other words, though they might have been the people closest to Alexander (i.e., the people most likely to know what he looked like and how to replicate that look one-for-one), they were officially employed by the king, meaning that whatever image Alexander wanted of himself to be presented was the image that they had to replicate. To put it in the simplest words possible, they were most likely not allowed to show him looking ugly. And unless we locate Alexander's tomb and have access to his skeletal remains, we won't be able to do a proper facial reconstruction and have at least an idea of what the Macedonian king might have looked like.

Based on the sculptures, we do see some common traits that appear throughout. For example, Alexander would almost always look up in nearly every statue, suggesting that he might have been a bit short. In addition, his face is always tilted, which might have either been from birth or a result of a neck injury during the battle (and indeed, there are reports of him injuring his neck several times during his many conquests). The empty gaze in his eyes and the constant half-open mouth might even suggest a hint of a mental deficiency, perhaps even a light form of autism. However, based on his actions, this assessment is impossible to conclude one way or the other.

Strikingly, every single statue, painting, and mosaic depicts Alexander with wavy, lion-like hair, a thin hawkish nose, and bulging piercing eyes. His forehead also tends to jut out significantly. These traits suggest that Alexander might not have been the most attractive individual in Macedon during his youth, and if we take that theory to heart, it would also explain why he would tilt his head in nearly every portrait as if to minimize the impact of his forehead and eyes.

Regarding his upper and lower body, he is almost always depicted as rather muscular and well built, a standard practice for heroes and generals in the Hellenic world. Whether he was exactly as "chiseled" as his statues are is up for debate. However, considering he was Macedonian royalty, he must have been trained in combat and hunting, which would certainly keep his body in peak physical condition. Furthermore, his quick marches and readiness to go head-first into battle suggest that he had a lot of stamina, something that only a physically fit individual might have. Of course, it's possible that his physique worsened over time, especially due to overeating, overdrinking, and mourning over the losses of his loved ones, Hephaestion in particular. Early signs of stress and even potential post-traumatic stress disorder could have very well been an everyday problem for the young king.

Interestingly, some sources note that Alexander's eyes were heterochromatic, i.e., the color of one was different from the other. While that isn't a common trait, it still happens often enough today, and it wasn't even out of the ordinary in the ancient world. However, the eye detail could have simply been something added by an ancient biographer in order to make Alexander stand out further.

Roman copy of the original statue of Alexander the Great found in Alexandria, circa 3ᵈ century BCE

Alexander's Traits

Alexander grew up as a prince, but more importantly, he grew up mainly under the influence of his mother. With Philip constantly warring and court intrigue being very much an everyday occurrence for the boy, Alexander could have easily grown to resent his father, even well past Philip's death. Most of the accounts of Alexander that even remotely mention Philip emphasize how much the two were at odds and how much Alexander wanted to put distance between him and Philip. Obviously, that might have been an exaggeration on the part of the ancient authors, but it's not impossible to think that Alexander wanted more out of his father.

It was through his mother that Alexander saw himself as a direct descendant of the ancient Greek heroes, which might have led to the development of a superiority complex. And considering he grew up in nobility, wanting for very little, this newfound complex, coupled with the desire to own more and conquer more, could very well have been his driving force, more than any real Pan-Hellenic or even purely Macedonian ideals. Simply put, Alexander had an image of himself as great before he even got the sobriquet Great.

The influence of Olympias, however, might have dug even deeper than the tales of his heritage. It wouldn't be out of the ordinary that Alexander developed a desire to be validated by mother figures throughout his life, an early form of an Oedipus complex. His treatment of Darius's mother is a perfect example of that, but it's far from the only one. Queen Ada's adoption of Alexander as her son also plays well into this notion.

In terms of specific traits, we can assume some of them were simply based on his dealings with his supporters and his opponents during battles or political intrigue. For example, Alexander was shown as prudent and calculating in terms of who he would spare and who he would support. He wasn't beyond pardoning even the worst offenders, and his companion Harpalus was the perfect example of that. Harpalus, who was lame in the leg, would not follow Alexander through his campaign but would receive a post in Asia Minor. He was known to be fond of stealing and absconded with Alexander's money a grand total of three times, two of those times being pardoned by the Macedonian king. In terms of sparing his enemies, though possibly a political maneuver to keep the locals in check, Alexander did what most conquerors did; if the ruler recognized him as king, he would retain his post unharmed and would even receive honors. If, however, the person refused to do that, Alexander would punish them, and he was exceptionally brutal in dispensing punishments.

Being raised as a member of royalty, Alexander was not immune to a bit of court intrigue himself, being more than willing to remove those people who threatened his position. Attalus was just one prominent example and perhaps not as important as that of Parmenion and his son Philotas. In 330, Philotas was accused of conspiring to kill Alexander, after which he was promptly captured, tortured until he admitted to the plot, then executed. Whether he was guilty of the plot or not didn't really matter to Alexander, nor did it matter if Parmenion was involved or not. At the time, Parmenion was leading his own section of the army, with Alexander having divided it prior to the battle with the Uxians. Alexander ordered two men, Cleander and Sitalces, to rush to where Parmenion was and execute him, which they did not long after. Of course, the murder of Parmenion might have appeared rash to some, but Alexander might have simply been looking for a reason to remove the general. After all, Parmenion had been in service since Philip was king, and though significantly older than Alexander, he was still a capable soldier with enormous local support. Furthermore, had he learned of his son's death, he might have easily turned against the Macedonian king and staged a successful coup.

Ancient authors and some modern historians suggest that Alexander might have been prone to outbursts of rage and that he might have even become somewhat of an alcoholic in his later years. Indeed, the famous episode of him killing Cleitus the Black with a spear during one drunken argument (and Alexander's reaction of sadness and disappointment about his actions) has fueled this notion for more than two millennia. However, by analyzing his exploits, we can safely assume that the outbursts of rage were not particularly common, and when they did happen, not all of them included alcohol. In fact, when he wanted to end Bessus for killing Darius or when he wanted to exact vengeance on the guards of the tomb of Cyrus the Great at the city of Pasargadae who desecrated the grave, he was perfectly sober. In addition, his supposed alcoholism also has to be questioned, considering he never showed any craving for alcohol akin to how a true addict might. More than likely, Alexander's excessive drinking only came with important events, such as successful conquests, banquets, dinners, and weddings.

While Alexander most certainly could read and write, and while he was a great admirer of the written word, he wasn't much of an intellectual. Most of his actions show him to be a doer rather than a thinker, someone who would not spend hours pondering over a philosophical idea. Nevertheless, his interest in the sciences at the time was evident, as was his admiration of the arts. Not only would he keep a personal historian, artist, sculptor, and actor around, but he would frequently commission his subjects to organize lavish games and festivals full of dancing, poetry readings, and sports.

Alexander's Beliefs and Motivations

It's incredibly difficult to piece together a profile of a historical figure that lived more than two thousand years ago, especially when the scant few historical accounts of him offer some wildly different and even contradictory facts about him. And indeed, it's just as hard to figure out what drove this individual to commit the acts that he did. It's slightly easier to do with contemporary figures or even figures from almost a century ago (like Hitler, Stalin, Lenin, Mao, etc.), considering the wealth of sources and the immediacy of the events, but if we step as little as a century earlier, we run into stumbling blocks and gaps of information. So, how do we assess Alexander the Great in this way, a man who has been dead since 323 BCE and whose contemporaries appeared to have different stances on him?

Well, it would be instructive to only use the most agreed-upon events and start building a character profile from there. We know that both his parents had an influence on him, though in wildly different ways. From his mother's side, Alexander would have learned that her side of the family draws a direct lineage from Achilles, which would have no doubt built up his ego. We often find in descriptions of Alexander's travels that he wanted to emulate the feats of both Achilles and Heracles, and later on, we see him eschew Greek gods and heroes in place of Persian and Egyptian ones. In fact, at one point during his life, he was openly deified as a living god, a practice not uncommon among the ancient peoples at the time (even Greeks did it on occasion). So, it's safe to say that Alexander wanted to see himself as, if not an outright god, at least a divine hero or a heroic figure to honor his supposed ancestors. Of course, the whole thing could have simply been a clever political maneuver to legitimize himself as an all-Greek hero and a rightful hegemon of the League of Corinth, but again, that's up for speculation.

The influence from his father was a bit more passive and less direct than that of his mother. Philip did not engage with Alexander directly during his childhood, so the only time the boy saw him was on the battlefield. As shown earlier, Philip was an excellent strategist, a cunning diplomat, and a ruthless warrior, and most of those traits rubbed off of him and stuck with Alexander. The boy would show promise as early as a sixteen-year-old, and even today, there are few heads of state that have accomplished so much by their early twenties (the same age Alexander took the throne). But what exactly motivated

Alexander to pursue warfare so much that it nearly cost him his troops' loyalty and his own life multiple times? Well, most ancient scholars assume it was the envy of his father and jealousy of his success, and if we were to be Freudian about it, maybe even a need for validation. Alexander had his moments when he praised his father, like the time he told the nobles of Macedon that it was Philip who took them from the mountains to the plains and civilized them. But overall, his dealings with Philip saw the two at odds, with Alexander angry at his father for not recognizing his greatness and potential. Furthermore, dynastic struggles were a common occurrence even back then, so Philip's seventh marriage could have had a serious impact on the young man.

Of course, Philip would die well before Alexander even set foot on Asian soil, so we can't pin everything Alexander did to something as simple as "he wanted to outdo Philip." His conquest was inarguably his greatest living achievement, and while it may have started as a Pan-Hellenic crusade, it certainly did not continue nor, indeed, end like one. So, as a young man and an inheritor of the hegemony over the Greeks, Alexander might have initially been an advocate of a Pan-Hellenic union. After all, most of his teachers were not Macedonian; the majority of them were Greek, not to mention that his favorite works of fiction came from Greek authors as well. But that goal might have gradually shifted along the lines of "union of all Greeks/destruction of Persia/conquest of the Persian Empire/inheriting the Persian Empire/building a new empire under his name with a new race of people governing it." Hunger for power is a trait all conquerors seem to share, and at some point, idealism outweighs pragmatism. Of course, the thrill of new conquest and the hunger for war (or even the good, old-fashioned hunger for the plunder of war) could have been the main motivation, especially if we consider that Alexander did a lot of conquering but exceptionally little consolidating. That's where he fell short of Philip's genius; as a seasoned veteran, Philip knew that simply taking a city over and installing your own vassal there wasn't enough. You had to engage with the people there and convince them that the transition of power, though bloody and initially nasty, would be a net benefit for them in the long run. In fact, even the people Alexander admired, like Cyrus the Great of the Achaemenid dynasty, knew this, and he famously respected the customs and religions of every single region he conquered while maintaining the national identity of his native Persians, a trait for which he has remained known to this day. Alexander did indeed follow this line of reasoning to an extent but nowhere near as much as his father or his idol did. If anything, the mere fact that he wanted to supersede the customs of both the Macedonians and the Persians with the mass wedding speaks volumes in and of itself. More importantly, Alexander was not beyond destroying the cities that did him wrong and founding his own and imposing the Macedonian culture there; his destruction of Thebes and the razing of Persepolis are perfect examples.

In terms of belief, it's hard to pinpoint if Alexander was a truly religious man, at least in the modern sense. He might have been prone to superstition, as were most rulers back in ancient times, but it's interesting to note just how often his beliefs changed, ranging from paying tribute to Greek gods and heroes to worshiping an Egyptian deity and accepting Persian religious customs. His own deification might have also been a new development that he either readily accepted or simply didn't pay much heed to. Considering Alexander's age and the extraordinary events of his life, it would not be out of the ordinary to see his conquests as containing an element of religious "soul-searching" that most men in their twenties and thirties go through. It would be the equivalent of a modern man coming from a religious household, then rebelling and turning to atheism in his early and late teens, becoming radicalized and going extreme in his twenties and thirties, and then choosing an unrelated religion and devoting himself to it in his middle years. Alexander's case would, however, be more extreme than that if this chain of events applies to him, considering he crossed thousands of miles, conquered hundreds of cities, towns, and villages, and came into contact with different, sometimes wildly contrasting cultures with religious beliefs that often contradicted those of their neighbors.

Chapter 6 – Myths of Alexander: Select Stories from the Alexander Romance

With a figure as accomplished as Alexander, it's no surprise that a myriad of myths and legends would form, making him out to be an almost mythical figure of divine power. It's a practice that has surprisingly stayed strong even to this day, with politicians, generals, and even ordinary everyday people being deified for specific deeds and supernatural legends being built around them. Most of the accounts of Alexander's fantastical exploits were collected in one work dubbed the *Alexander Romance* (though due to its complexity and history, some historians and literary scholars suggest that it's not so much a single piece of work but rather an entire genre in and of itself).

The *Alexander Romance* was written, at least initially, with the intention of serving as a historical account of Alexander's exploits, but only the core of the story (i.e., the various historical events) can be attested as true to some extent. Everything else built around them is fiction. Furthermore, even when the original Greek text was compiled (sometime before 338 CE, when the first Latin translation appeared), authors who copied the text added their own segments to the original and greatly expanded it. Some early versions of the *Alexander Romance* have been translated into Coptic, Arabic, Armenian, Syriac, and Hebrew, and depending on the region, the translated version would influence later editions (and later additions).

What follows is a selection of some of the most interesting bits and pieces of the *Alexander Romance*, showing the scope and ingenuity of the ancient author in crafting the legend of the king of Macedon and making it plausible enough for the ancient mind to consider it as fact.

Alexander's Conception and Birth

To many, Alexander is known as the son of King Philip II of Macedon, a great leader and a man of few failings. But Alexander's greatness comes from a greater source, for his father was not really Philip. No, Alexander had different roots, those of Egyptian kings.

Indeed, the last of the great Egyptian kings, Nectanebo II, would be the man to father Alexander. After having divined the advances of the Persian army, with all of its many peoples charging toward Memphis, the great pharaoh fled and found himself in Macedon in the guise of a magician. Philip received the man kindly. At the time, he had no heir since Olympias had not yet borne him a son. Before embarking onto a new battle, Philip told Olympias, in no uncertain terms, that she had better bear him a son or she would no longer know his embrace. The queen summoned Nectanebo, who instantly fell for her, and sought his assistance. The pharaoh, as a mage, told her that in order to conceive a child, she would have to copulate with Amon of Libya, a god with a golden beard, golden hair, and huge horns of gold. He prophesied that Olympias would see him in her dreams, to which the queen responded, "If I see this dream, I shall reverence you not as a magician, but as a god."

Nectanebo divined some dream magic, causing Olympias to see the vision of which he spoke. He instructed her to give him a room close to her own, and that should the night come when a serpent enters her room, she should expel everyone out but keep the lamps lit. Then, disguising himself both as a serpent and as the god Amon, Nectanebo entered her chamber that night and made love to her, which she readily accepted, thinking he was the god Amon.

For days on end, Nectanebo would come and impregnate Olympias, and over time, her belly swelled with child. Worried that her husband might suspect adultery, the Macedonian queen asked Nectanebo for guidance. Once again, the pharaoh divined a spell wherein he sent a dream to Philip, a dream carried by a sea-hawk across the land and the waters. Philip, having dreamed of the god impregnating his wife, asked an interpreter about his dream, and the interpreter rejoiced, claiming that Philip's son would be born of Olympias but that he would also be the offspring of the gods.

Initially skeptical, Philip came back to see his wife, somewhat disturbed. He proceeded to calm her down and confirmed that the child indeed belonged to Amon. But it wouldn't be long until the king of Macedon accused his wife of having an affair with Nectanebo. The pharaoh overheard this, so during dinner one evening, he turned himself into a snake and crept into the dining room, in full view of everyone. The serpent hissed violently, but Olympias recognized the snake and extended her hand to it, which prompted the animal to calm down and lay its head in her lap. Philip and the others were stunned at this display, and they were equally stunned when the serpent turned into an eagle and flew away. Unsure of which god it was that spoke to him, whether it be Amon, Apollo, or Asclepius, Philip spoke to Olympias, and indeed, she confirmed it to be the Egyptian Amon who had impregnated her and bestowed upon Philip a worthy heir.

Philip would not be done seeing signs of his new son, however. In the palace gardens, the Macedonian king saw a bird lay an egg next to him. The egg rolled out and fell onto the ground. A serpent came out, rapidly making a circle around the egg and proceeding to come back to it, only to end up dead with its head just barely entering the yolk. An interpreter spoke to Philip about this gruesome scene, letting him know that his son would circle the world but would die before coming back to his homeland. Soon enough, Olympias was ready to give birth, and Nectanebo was right there by her side, divining according to the position of the planets and the stars. And it was on that day, among thunder, lightning, and the shaking of the earth itself, that the new ruler of Macedon, an Egyptian ruler by birth, would be born, and that ruler would be Alexander.

Alexander Kills Nectanebo

Alexander was born with hair akin to a lion's mane, asymmetrical eyes, teeth as sharp as nails, and movements as swift as those of a lion. He was educated in ways of philosophy, language, mathematics, and war, and he would go on to be such a successful pupil that he would tutor his own peers shortly after. He wore armor, marched with the troops, and was a prodigy in terms of warfare. Philip adored the boy, but he did not like the fact that Alexander looked nothing like him. "I love your character and nobility, Alexander, but not your appearance because you in no way resemble me," Philip said.

Worried, Olympias asked Nectanebo to find out what Philip was planning with the boy. So, one day, when Alexander was twelve years of age, he was sitting near Olympias and Nectanebo, studying the stars. He asked the wizard if he could learn of the stars in heaven, to which the Egyptian replied that they would have to wait for nightfall. Nightfall came, and Nectanebo took Alexander away from the city to a secluded area where the child could see the stars. However, Alexander pushed Nectanebo into a deep pit, where the wizard broke his neck. Puzzled, Nectanebo asked Alexander why he did it, to which the boy replied that the mathematician had only himself to blame. "Because," the boy said, "although you do not understand earthly matters, you investigate those of heaven."

It would be then that Nectanebo unveiled to Alexander that they were one kin, that prophecy had foretold of the Egyptian pharaoh being killed by his progeny. Alexander was grief-stricken to learn that he had just killed his own father, so he pulled him out of the pit and carried his body back to Pella, to his mother's shock. Olympias felt like a fool for being tricked into laying with Nectanebo, but nevertheless, she gave the pharaoh a princely burial. It is, indeed, somewhat ironic that an Egyptian ruler was to rest forever in a Macedonian tomb, whereas a Macedonian ruler, who would be his son, was to rest forever in an Egyptian one.

Alexander Tames Bucephalas

When Alexander was twelve years of age, a colt was born of exceptional beauty within Philip's stables. However, it was a man-eater and incredibly wild. Philip's stablemen brought up the issue with the Macedonian king, and he ordered the colt be kept in an iron cage without a bridle, stating that whosoever commits a grave sin against the king will be thrown to the horse as punishment. "Truly then the proverb of the Greeks is fulfilled, that good grows very close to evil," the king said. He noted that the horse had a mark on its haunch that looked like an ox-head.

Years later, Philip would go to Delphi to consult the oracle on who would be king after him. The Pythia (the high priestess) took a sip from the Castalian spring and spoke her words, claiming that whosoever rides the ox-head horse bridleless through Pella will be the next king, a king who will come to rule the world.

When Alexander turned fifteen, he passed next to the horse's iron cage one day, and the animal whinnied at the sound of his voice. When the boy asked about the horse, Ptolemy, Philip's general, said that the horse had to be locked up because it was eating people. But the minute the boy spoke again, the horse whinnied some more, with a submissive tone of a faithful companion. Alexander approached the horse, which proceeded to lick the boy, acknowledging him as its master. Alexander set the horse free and grabbed its mane, climbing up onto it without a bridle and riding it through the city. When Philip learned of this, he was overjoyed, remembering the prophecy at Delphi. He embraced his son, claiming that he would be the king of kings and the ruler of the world.

Alexander and a Drunken Philip

Alexander participated in a chariot race and took the victory one time. After coming back to share his achievements with his parents, he learned that Philip had spurned Olympias and took a new woman as his wife, one Cleopatra, daughter of Lysias. Alexander was not happy with this news, stating to his father that he offered his crown of victory and that once he gave his mother Olympias's hand in marriage to another king, he would invite Philip to the wedding. Both father and son were now angry at each other, seated across one another at the table, with Alexander refusing to drink.

During the dinner, a drunken Lysias proclaimed his support for King Philip, and in doing so, he asked the gods to provide Philip and Cleopatra a legitimate heir, one that did not come from adultery and that bore a resemblance to Philip. Alexander overheard this, and in a fit of rage, he threw his goblet at the noble, killing him on the spot. Angry, Philip stumbled to hit Alexander but tripped on the edge of his couch and fell over.

Alexander mocked him publicly for this stunt. "You are eager to conquer all Asia and to destroy Europe to its foundations," the boy proclaimed, referring to his father's grandiose plans to crush Persia and unite the Hellenes, "yet you are unable to take a single step without stumbling." Cleopatra was sent into exile shortly after, and Philip was taken away and laid to bed in order to rest.

Alexander and Diogenes

Diogenes was a famed cynic philosopher, originally from Sinope in Ionia, who had been living in Corinth when Alexander was consolidating his empire. Throughout his life, Diogenes had been a controversial individual, publicly mocking those in power without remorse and with a sharp, unyielding tongue.

When Alexander was in Corinth, the young hegemon saw many philosophers approach him and heap praise upon him, but the son of Philip had expected Diogenes to appear, as he was a fan of his rhetoric. Diogenes, however, could not have cared less for the Macedonian ruler, opting not to even give him the time of day. Alexander, proactive as he was, sought to find Diogenes himself and enjoy his company.

At one point, Alexander managed to find Diogenes, who was relaxing in the sunlight, leaned against a barrel. "Who are you?" the young hegemon asked.

"This, your majesty, is Diogenes the philosopher," the people around Alexander said, no doubt frightened of the old man's indifference to the ruler of all Greeks, "who so often advised the Athenians to fight against your power."

Alexander, possibly overjoyed in finally locating the famed philosopher, approached Diogenes a bit closer. "Diogenes," the young monarch asked, "what favor can I do for you?"

"Nothing," replied the philosopher, "except to go away and leave me the sunshine so that I can warm myself."

Alexander was quite amused by this response, bold and brash as it was, for it fit Diogenes's personality perfectly. "Truly," the young king said, "if I were not Alexander, then I should wish to be Diogenes."

"If I were not Diogenes, I would still wish to be Diogenes," the philosopher concluded.

Alexander at Gordium

It was in the early years of Alexander's conquests that he arrived at the city of Gordium, the capital of Phrygia. At one point in history, the city had no king, so the oracle declared that the next person to drive into the city on an ox-cart would be declared king, and that person was a man named Gordias. His son, Midas, dedicated the ox-cart to the god Sabazios and tied it to a post with an intricate and complex knot.

When Alexander arrived at Gordium, Phrygia no longer had a king but was a satrapy of the Persian Empire. The new legend proclaimed that anyone who could loosen the Gordian knot would become ruler of all Asia. Feeling up to the challenge, Alexander went on to try and loosen the knot, unable to do so at first. However, at one point, the young king declared that it made no difference how the knot was untied as long as it was loose. With those words uttered, Alexander pulled out his sword and hacked at the knot, letting the cornel bark drop onto the ground after a single stroke. It was indeed as prophecy had foretold, for Alexander went on to conquer everything up to the Indian lands, effectively becoming the lord of Asia.

Alexander cuts the Gordian knot, painted by Giovanni Paolo Pannini between 1718 and 1719

Alexander in Libya

Once most of coastal Asia Minor was his, Alexander set out to Libya, seeking the Oracle of Amon. He ordered his army to leave and to sail to the island of Proteus and wait for him there, for he wanted to enter the god's sanctuary by himself. After entering, he began to pray to Amon, asking him, "Oh, mighty Amon, is it true what my mother Olympias had told me? Is it true that I am your son?" And thus, Amon appeared to Alexander in a vision, embracing Olympias and saying to him, "Alexander, my child, you are indeed born of my seed."

Alexander proceeded to repair the old sanctuary of Amon, gilding his wooden statue and erecting it with an inscription that read, "Alexander erected this to his father, the mighty god Amon." Before leaving, he prayed to Amon once again, asking if he should found a new city and where he should do it. Another vision of Amon came to him, an old man with ram's horns on his temples and golden hair. The vision spoke to Alexander, stating that he should found the city across the isle of Proteus, a city that would endure a thousand generations and celebrate his name. Alexander gave thanks to Amon, making another sacrifice in his name, then went on to rest at a certain village in Libya where his troops had rested some days before.

Alexander and the Siege of Tyre

Upon coming back from Libya, Alexander sought to besiege the fortified city of Tyre. The Tyrians knew that if a king was to come seeking conquest, their city would be leveled to the ground, as it had been foretold by an oracle. Thus, the Tyrians fought tooth and nail for their city, and many Macedonians died in the fray, with Alexander having to accept defeat and withdraw to Gaza. Angry at this defeat, Alexander was plotting his next attack when, in a dream, a voice told him not to visit the city as a messenger. Taking the dream as a bad omen, Alexander instead sent several messengers of his own, with a message that sought either a peaceful surrender from the Tyrians or a swift and brutal death. And upon their arrival, the messengers were asked by the Tyrians, "Which one of you is Alexander?" They replied that none of them was the young king, and the Tyrians crucified them and displayed them on the city walls. Alexander was enraged at this display but still could not attack without knowing if he would win or not.

One night, a dream came to Alexander, a dream of a satyr giving him a curd cheese. Alexander took this cheese and trampled it under his foot ferociously. Upon waking up, the king asked for an interpreter to explain the meaning of this dream to him and learned that it was a good omen, that Tyre would be his. Emboldened by these words, Alexander employed the help of men from the three neighboring villages in Libya that had assisted him during the original siege, villages where his army had previously camped. The men entered Tyre by night, opened the gates, and killed as many guards as possible. Alexander marched through the city gates, and a huge battle ensued. The Tyrians were utterly defeated, and their city was sacked and leveled to the ground.

Alexander would reward the men of the three villages that helped him. To this day, a city he erected stands in place of those three villages, aptly named Tripolis.

Alexander and the Letter of Darius

Darius had sent a letter to Alexander while the Macedonian king was in Tyre. Aside from the letter, the Persian king had sent a whip, a ball, and a chest of gold. These were his words to Alexander:

The King of Kings who rises into heavens Darius, to my servant Alexander, I order you to go back to your home in Macedon and be my slave, to rest in the lap of your mother, and to play with your peers. You are at an age where you still need to be nursed, after all. I have thus sent a whip, a ball, and a chest of gold. The whip is to show that you would still obey; the ball was so you and your peers would play at home instead of you recruiting them, making of them arrogant and violent young men who do nothing but senselessly destroy. Even if you were to all unite under one man, you could not defeat the mighty Persian Empire. I have so many troops that counting them would be like counting grains of sand on a beach, and I have more than enough gold and silver to fill the whole world. Thus I have sent a chest of gold as well so that you can pay your bandits what they need to go back home. If you obey these orders, you will be safe. If you refuse, however, I shall send my men so they can pursue and capture you, and then you shall not be treated as the son of Philip but as a rebel and a slave.

Though his troops were terrified of this threat, Alexander assured them that these were but empty words from Darius, that his boastfulness was akin to a dog who has a loud bark but a weak bite. He then proceeded to have the messengers captured and tortured. When they pleaded for mercy, Alexander told them to blame their king of kings for speaking to Alexander as if he was some common thug and not a monarch. But when the messengers pleaded further, acknowledging Alexander's might and Darius's ignorance, Alexander let them go, showing them the difference between a Greek and a Persian king and how he, a non-barbarian, does not kill messengers.

Three days would pass, and Alexander wrote his own letter to Darius as a response:

King Alexander, son of king Philip and queen Olympias, greets the mighty king of kings seated on the throne just below the heavens. It is a great shame that someone as powerful as the king of Persians would fall so low as to be the slave of Alexander. For you bear the name of the gods before you, yet you do not honor that name, but merely wear it as a garment, for we have learned that you are powerless. I come to make war against you as a mortal against another mortal, yet the balance of victory is in the hands of the Providence above.

You boast of your gold and silver. Why? So we can fight over it more ferociously? As you have said, if I were to defeat you, I would have defeated a god on Earth, a wealthy king of kings that rules all of Persia, an achievement to be sure. But if you were to beat me, it would mean nothing—I am but a common bandit, after all, according to your own words.

The whip, the ball, and the chest of gold you sent me were gifts in mockery. Yet I openly accept them. I accept the whip, for I will use it to flay the barbarian troops with my own hands. I accept the ball, for it represents the whole round of the Earth, which I intend to rule. And that chest of gold you sent is a great sign of the things to come—for you will be my vassal and pay me tribute.

When Darius received his letter, he sent for his satraps to join him in battle, only for them to tell him how ferocious and cunning Alexander was in his conquest. Angered by this, Darius swore to bring an end to the young Macedonian king himself.

Alexander and the Temple of Apollo

Upon arriving at Acragas in Sicily, Alexander stormed into the temple of the god Apollo and asked the priestess for an oracle. The priestess replied that the god would not give him an oracle, which angered the young Macedonian king. He demanded the oracle again, but this time, he threatened to carry the tripod outside of the temple, in much the same way Heracles carried out the tripod of the temple of Phoebus, dedicated to the king of the Lydian Croesus. It was at that moment that the booming voice of the god came from deep within the temple itself. "Heracles, O Alexander, committed this act as one god against another; but you are mortal; do not oppose yourself to the gods. Your actions are talked of even as far away as heaven." The priestess spoke to Alexander again, this time in reverence, stating that the god had given Alexander the highest of honors in how he addressed him, as "Heracles, O Alexander." "Thus," she said, "you are to exceed all other men with your deeds, and your legend will be the one to outlive many generations."

Alexander and the Bridge of Euphrates

Alexander and his army were about to cross into Media, aiming to take the Greater Armenian lands. However, before them stood the mighty Euphrates, as swift as the fastest horse and as deep and treacherous as an ocean. The Macedonian king ordered his troops to build a bridge with iron arches over the river so that they could all cross and push onward. However, once the bridge was complete, his troops were hesitant to go across, fearing that the bridge might give way and that they would plummet to their deaths. Alexander ordered that they send their beasts of burden and wagons with provisions first, but still, the soldiers would not go across. Electing to lead by example, the young conqueror crossed the bridge first, and soon enough, his emboldened men followed.

As soon as the last man made it across, Alexander ordered them to dismantle the bridge. Shocked, the soldiers pleaded with Alexander not to pursue this order, claiming that they might need it to cross the river again to safety should the barbarians advance.

"Fellow soldiers," he stated, giving a speech to everyone present, "you are filling me with confidence of victory with all of your talk about retreat and defeat. It was for this very reason that I ordered you to dismantle that bridge we crossed, so that when you fight, you will win, and so that you would not be defeated and then turn your tail to run. War is won not by the one who flees but by the one who pursues. When we all win, we shall return to Macedon together; battle is like play to us."

Emboldened by his words, the army praised Alexander and marched onward to war.

Alexander and the Persian Soldier

After crossing the Euphrates, Alexander's troops made camp, but they were not aware that Darius's men also had an encampment there. Fighting ensued, and bravery was found on both sides. At one point, a Persian soldier, dressed in Macedonian garb, approached Alexander from behind and struck the back of his head, cracking his skull. He was promptly captured and taken to the Macedonian king in chains.

"Soldier, why did you do that to your own king?" Alexander asked the man before him.

"Do not be deceived, O king of Macedon," the man replied, "for though I may wear Macedonian garb, I am a Persian. I asked my king what he was willing to give me should I give him your head, and he promised me a part of his kingdom and his daughter's hand in marriage. I intended to strike you dead but have missed the mark, and now, here I stand before you, a man in chains."

To the astonishment of many, Alexander ordered the Persian man to be released and let go unharmed. He then turned to his troops. "You, too, men of Macedon, must strive to be as brave as this man I have just released."

Alexander at the Sogdian Rock

Alexander had reached the famed Sogdian Rock, a fortress deemed impenetrable and thus unable to be conquered. He asked the men of the Sogdian Rock to surrender to him, yet their only reply was that he would need men with wings if he were to capture their fortress.

Alexander did not give up. He spoke to his troops, asking for volunteers who had experience in climbing. Some three hundred men reported for duty, and he had them all use metal tent pegs and strong flaxen linens to climb the Rock. They would do so under the darkness of night, and some thirty brave men lost their lives during the climb.

As they were reaching the summit, they were to wave their linen down at the ground as a signal. Alexander then sent a messenger to the Rock, and the messenger spoke to the citizens there. "If you were to look down, O men of the Rock," the messenger said, "you would see that our king has found his winged men." And indeed, the linen waving in the wind reminded the men of the Sogdian Rock of wings, and they were terrified of Alexander's advance, so they surrendered quickly. It would be here that Alexander would meet and fall in love with Roxane, who would bear him an heir years later.

Alexander and Roxane, engraving based on a drawing by Raffaello Sanzio 16ᵗʰ century[xii]

Alexander and the Two Trees (Prophecy of His Death #1)

While campaigning in India, Alexander came to the city of Prasiake, the capital of all of India and the home of the late King Porus. Once there, he was greeted by the wise men of the kingdom, who heaped praise upon him. However, one group approached him and asked to show him something of interest. They claimed that there were two trees that spoke in human voices within the Temple of the Sun and the Moon and that Alexander had to hear their message to him. And indeed, when Alexander entered the temple, two trees not unlike cypresses stood there. They were surrounded by a myriad of other trunks resembling either fruit trees or myrrh-nut trees. One tree spoke with a man's voice and was surrounded by male animal skins; this tree was named the Sun. The other tree spoke with a woman's voice and was surrounded by female animal skins; this tree was named the Moon. Around them, there was no tin, bronze, iron, or clay. The wise men told Alexander that if he were pure, he could enter the temple, make obeisance, and wait, and the trees would speak to him and provide him with an oracle. No iron was allowed in the temple, so

Alexander's troops left their weapons outside. Some Indian men also accompanied Alexander, and he promised them that, should he not receive any oracle, they would be burned alive.

The trees both spoke three times, the Sun tree during the day, the Moon tree during the night. They would speak once when their star was rising, once more when it was at its peak, and the final time as it was setting. And indeed, as the sun set, the Sun tree's voice spoke in Indian, and its message was such that the Indian companions of Alexander were afraid to translate it. After the king pushed them to do so, they claimed that he would soon be killed by one of his closest companions. Alexander, disturbed by this news, asked the tree for another oracle, demanding to know whether he would see his mother Olympias again and embrace her. The moon then rose, and the Moon tree spoke in a female voice, in Greek this time. "Alexander," it said, "you are destined to die in Babylon. You will never again enter Macedon, and you will never embrace your mother Olympias again."

Alexander and Kalanos (Prophecy of His Death #2)

Among Alexander's Indian subjects from Taxila was a certain Kalanos, a gymnosophist who lived an ascetic life and considered even food and clothing as sinful. The seventy-three-year-old felt weakened by all the marching that Alexander's troops did, and he told the young conqueror that he preferred to die than to live as an invalid. He asked to self-immolate, which disturbed the men around him. Ultimately, the task of immolation fell onto Alexander's general Ptolemy. The pyre was to be lit in Susa.

Kalanos distributed his costly gifts, the same ones he got from Alexander, to all the people present, choosing to dress himself in a simple garland and to chant Vedic hymns. His horse was gifted to Lysimachus, one of his pupils and Alexander's trusted officers. Alexander himself was not present to see the old man burn.

And the old man did burn, yet he did not flinch a single time, much to the amazement of many. His final words, however, were directed at the absent Alexander, and he simply said, "We shall meet in Babylon." Upon his death, messengers went to Alexander to let him know of his fate. Alexander did not understand the meaning of these words, having no plans of going to Babylon at the time. Yet, these words would prove to be true, as, during that same year, the young king would forever depart the world of the living, and it would indeed be in Babylon.

Alexander's Will

When the illness fell upon Alexander, he decided to produce a will, whereupon he decreed who would succeed him, who would take the helm of the many territories of his empire, and how his wealth would be distributed. A section of his will addresses the many territories he gained, and in terms of succession, he wrote thus:

I have appointed Craterus (the regent of Macedon), Ptolemy (the satrap of Egypt), Antigonus and Perdiccas to control the regions of Asia. Do not ignore these orders, for it is your own duty to lead these lands and make them prosper.

I appoint my half-brother Arrhidaeus, son of Philip, as king of Macedon for the time being, but should my consort Roxane produce a male heir, he is to inherit my throne as king of Macedon. Should Roxane produce a female child, then let the Macedonians choose whomsoever they want to as king, but let the new ruler pay homage to the Argeads and celebrate us as the customs demand it. My mother, Olympias, is to live in Rhodes, but only if both she and the Rhodians agree to this arrangement. If not, she is free to live wherever she likes.

As stated earlier, Craterus is to act as regent of Macedonia, alongside his wife Cynane, the daughter of Philip, my father; Lysimachus and his wife Thesalonike, daughter of Philip, my father, are to rule over Thrace; Leonnatos and his wife Cleodice, the sister of Olcias, are to rule over the satrapy of the Hellespont; Eumenes,

Alexander's secretary, is to rule over Paphlagonia and Cappadocia; Antigonus is to rule Pamphylia and Cilicia, as far as the Halys River; Seleucus is to rule over Babylon; Meleager will take Hollow Syria and Phoenicia; Perdiccas will reign over Egypt; Ptolemy will rule over Libya alongside his wife Cleopatra, the sister of Alexander; regions beyond Babylon will fall under Phanocrates and his wife Roxane the Bactrian; the islanders will reign over themselves, with Rhodes as their chief island.

As with the Indian lands, those as far as the Hydaspes River will be ruled by Taxiles, king of India; Porus will be King of all India beyond the Hydaspes; Oxydrakes of Bactria, father of Roxane my consort, will reign over Paropanisadae; (What proceeds is another list of lands and its appointed rulers, most of whom are missing due to the lacuna in the original text.)

Upon hearing his will read out loud, Ptolemy asked Alexander to whom he was leaving his kingdom. "To him who is strong, who is willing, who can keep it, and who can maintain it," Alexander replied.

Chapter 7 – Alexander's Legacy: Division of His Empire and His Successors

It should really shock no one that Alexander's empire began falling apart almost immediately after his death in 323. After all, he was not good at consolidating his subjects, and none of the main nations of nobility within the empire—neither the Macedonians nor the Greeks nor the Persians—respected or even tolerated each other. In fact, the very next year, almost every single marriage conducted at Susa was nullified, with Seleucus being probably the sole example to the contrary, at least among the elites. The fact that Alexander had no heir yet presented a problem as well. The only real candidate who could take the Macedonian throne was his half-brother, Arrhidaeus, who was mentally unstable. Indeed, it was up to Alexander's closest allies and generals to maintain the huge, vast empire, and they did so the only way they knew how—by breaking it apart and warring against each other for supremacy.

These men, the former generals and companions of Alexander, would come to be known to history as the Successors, or the Diadochi. And while their actions would amount to little else other than deplorable, they would come to found some of the greatest dynasties in southeastern Europe, northeastern Africa, and the Middle East. In fact, remnants of those empires would remain well nearing the end of the 1st century BCE, and they would come into contact with the new European hegemon, Rome.

The histories of all of these kingdoms are complex and convoluted, but they all had to stem from somewhere. They had to have a man who would act as the progenitor of the dynasty, and those men were all close to Alexander, figuratively (and, in a few cases, quite literally) using his corpse to justify their own legitimacy.

Antipater

Antipater, one of the oldest people at Alexander's court, was at first the advisor of King Philip II, a title he kept when Alexander took the throne. When the young king first crossed into Asia, he made Antipater the regent of Macedon in his absence, and indeed, Antipater would prove to be quite capable in handling the region, having staved off several rebellions and winning key battles, most notably the one against the Spartans in the Battle of Megalopolis in 330.

Antipater was a divisive figure, despite how effective he objectively was. Greeks and Macedonians didn't exactly respect him due to his support of tyrants like Philip and Alexander. Interestingly, Alexander himself might have grown jealous of Antipater's successes back in Macedon, dubbing his military exploits against the Spartans as a "battle of mice." Before his death, Alexander ordered Antipater to lead fresh troops in Asia and relinquish the regency over Macedon to Craterus, who was taking the demobilized veterans back from Asia Minor. Due to Alexander dying, Antipater was able to maintain his position, participating in the subsequent Lamian War and beating the rebellious Greeks at the Battle of Crannon in 322.

Antipater would have to ally with some of the Diadochi in what is commonly called the Wars of the Successors. He was a supporter of Craterus and Ptolemy, and they went up against Perdiccas and, more specifically, his ally Eumenes (one of the few Greeks to have a high position in Alexander's mostly Macedonian army during the king's life) in the Battle of the Hellespont in 321, a battle that saw Craterus die. Not long after, during the Treaty of Triparadeisos (a settlement in modern-day Lebanon), Antipater would be instrumental in helping divide the empire. He would remain the regent of Macedon, standing in for both Philip III and Alexander's infant son by Roxane, aptly named Alexander IV. A mere year later, in 320, he would fall ill, and a year after, he would die at the ripe age of eighty-one.

Interestingly, Antipater would end his life with similar consequences to those of Alexander, insofar as he caused a succession crisis. Antipater had a son, Cassander, who had been by his side throughout his career. However, thirty-six-year-old Cassander did not inherit the regency over Macedon; Antipater left that position to an old and seasoned war veteran named Polyperchon, which threw Cassander into a fit of rage and caused him to form an alliance with Antigonus the One-Eyed. Wars ensued between the son and the veteran, and in 317, Cassander would win. Ruling first as a regent, then as an outright king, Cassander would be the founder of the so-called Antipatrid dynasty, a house that was relatively short-lived compared to other Diadochi dynasties. They were crushed by the Antigonids a mere twenty-three years later.

Antigonus the One-Eyed

Antigonus I Monophthalmus, as he was called in Greek, was one of Philip's generals and a formidable warrior in his own time. He was a terrifying figure, made even worse considering the fact that he had only one eye, likely losing the other one in battle.

After Alexander's death, Antigonus, like so many other Diadochi, waged wars in order to maintain his territories. However, unlike most of the other Diadochi, Antigonus rarely lost a fight. In fact, he scored two major victories, one in the Battle of Orkynia and the other in the Battle of Cretopolis, against Perdiccas's supporters while being heavily outnumbered and disadvantaged.

Sometime around 306, during the Fourth War of the Diadochi, he declared himself and his son, Demetrius Poliorcetes, kings after the conquest of the island of Rhodes. Other Diadochi would follow his example later, and after Antigonus's death at the Battle of Ipsus in 301, his son would continue to rule, thus continuing the Antigonid dynasty, which would last for a few more centuries.

Seleucus I Nicator

Of all the Diadochi, Seleucus would hold the largest territory, claiming nearly all of Alexander's eastern lands up to India. At first, Seleucus was merely a satrap of Babylon, which still gave him vast territories to rule over (interestingly, he was one of the only nobles who did not divorce his Persian wife after the mass marriage at Susa), but he would inevitably be drawn to battle with the other Diadochi, notably losing against Antigonus and even withdrawing from Babylon at one time. When he returned to Babylon in 312, he would ruthlessly and effectively start conquering most of the surrounding territories once held by Alexander, and after a particular alliance with the Indian, or rather Mauryan, emperor Chandragupta (an alliance that provided Seleucus with more than five hundred war elephants), he would deal a crushing defeat to Antigonus at the Battle of Ipsus in 301. Twenty years later, he would also crush Lysimachus and add his territories to his kingdom.

Seleucus was an ambitious man who died at the ripe age of seventy-seven, assassinated by Ptolemy II Ceraunus, a deposed son of Ptolemy I Soter who sought refuge first with Lysimachus, then with Seleucus after he fled Egypt. Seleucus's son Antiochus would inherit the throne, thus continuing the Seleucid dynasty, one that would rule for more than two centuries before finally being deposed by the Romans in 63.

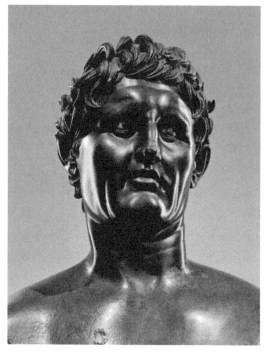

Roman bronze statue of Seleucus I Nicator, circa 100 BCE-100 CE[xiii]

Lysimachus

Like many of the Diadochi, Lysimachus, once a trusted bodyguard of Alexander (and a man who supposedly wrestled a lion he was trapped with, a deed that impressed the young Macedonian king), declared himself king in 306 and ruled over Thrace. However, unlike many of the other Diadochi, he would not found a dynasty that would last for centuries. Indeed, he would die in combat during the Battle of Corupedium, killed by Seleucus's troops.

Reportedly, Lysimachus was one of Alexander's favorite soldiers, earning distinction in many battles, especially during the Indian campaign. However, to his contemporaries, he was known as a vicious man who was not beyond killing his own children if he suspected them of conspiring against the throne.

Ptolemy I Soter

Ptolemy and his royal line, the Ptolemaic dynasty, would end up outliving the dynasties of nearly all the other Diadochi. After the death of Alexander, Ptolemy became the satrap of Egypt, a region he would later reign over as king.

As a ruler, Ptolemy accomplished much before his death, taking over Judea and parts of Syria, as well as Cyprus and Cyrenaica. More notably, he would be the one to consolidate Egypt and to found one of its most treasured institutions that was sadly lost to history, the famed Library of Alexandria. He would also marry multiple times, producing lots of potential heirs.

The Ptolemaic dynasty is, of course, known for its selection of noblewomen bearing the name Cleopatra. The one best known to history would be Cleopatra VII Philopator, the ruler of Egypt who would side with the Romans and the woman whose death marked the end of Ptolemaic Egypt and the beginning of Roman rule. Her death also symbolically marks the end of Hellenistic influence over the Mediterranean, seeing as she was the last independent ruler directly related to one of the Diadochi. Thus, the culture that came from Alexander the Great's time was slowly being replaced by that of Rome.

Depiction of Ptolemy I Soter as Pharaoh of Egypt, British Museum[iv]

Conclusion

Most of Alexander's life is steeped in legend, with talks of him descended from powerful gods and demigods, from heroes and men of valor, and while that does make for good storytelling, it's little more than myth. However, that doesn't take away from the greatness of Alexander, his deeds, and his impact.

Not long before his death, Alexander was worshiped as a god on Earth, and consequently, not long after his death, legends sprung up regarding his magnificent life. The Romans, in particular, tended to idolize the late Macedonian King of Kings, and though they would come to hold far more territory than he did, with much more efficiency in terms of running and consolidating the new lands, the people of the Roman Republic (and the subsequent empire) still looked up to Alexander as an idol of sorts. Early Christian and Muslim communities also deified him as a saint or a figure of interest, at the very least, and he even made it into other minor religions of every single region of the Old World where his name was known. And yes, he might have served as an inspiration to relatively modern generals and conquerors like Napoleon Bonaparte, but for Alexander, not too much time had to pass for him to become a cult figure. Indeed, people were worshiping him a few centuries before Jesus Christ was even conceived.

But myth is myth, and facts are facts. Ultimately, Alexander is a human being, albeit one born and raised in extraordinary surroundings. However, even if he didn't subdue a man-eating horse or meet the god Amon or speak to magical trees, he was still a force to be reckoned with. His military prowess rivaled and (maybe not so arguably) surpassed that of his father, and his swiftness to act has, in and of itself, become legendary. Few men could march as swiftly and efficiently as he did, and his first massive and quick lightning march was done when he was barely over twenty. In addition, he showed great adaptability on the battlefield and employed various tactics to subdue his opponents, including psychological warfare and using the terrain to his advantage. Obviously, he did not always succeed right away, as evidenced by the fact that some of his sieges would last for months, but his nearly perfect record in terms of victories speaks for itself.

And as is the case with every great ruler, Alexander had his flaws, and depending on whom you believe among the ancient authors, they range anywhere from mild character quirks to debilitating habits that would end most men's careers in a heartbeat. To some, he was an alcoholic and prone to fits of rage, and as a result, both his closest companions and his empire suffered for it. Yet to others, he was a soul who could listen to those he conquered and give them a second chance. Really, no single side is completely right or wrong here.

Alexander definitely had his episodes where even the most trusted devotees would despise him. And not all of his private affairs were all that savory, even to the ancient mind.

As stated earlier, results speak for themselves. During his reign, Alexander managed to crush a navy without using ships, an empire of millions with a proverbial handful of soldiers, and godlike opponents with nothing but his human wits (no matter how divine he thought his origins might have been). It was also thanks to him that Greekness, though disunited at home, became the dominant overlapping culture of the East for the next few centuries and whose effects would still be felt long after the last of the Diadochi dynasties were extinct. And it's here that things get a little speculative but also a little eerie—what if Alexander had lived ten years longer, or twenty, or more?

We can see, in the examples of Antipater, Antigonus, and Seleucus, that reaching maturity in terms of age, coupled with ever-evolving and unconventional war strategies, can produce spectacular results. Some of Alexander's plans involved subduing more of the Balkans and taking over the Arabian Peninsula, as well as pushing farther into India. What if he had met the tribes of central and eastern Europe? What if he had come into contact with the many different Chinese states (which, interestingly enough, Rome would do at one point) or even beyond that? Would his empire stretch all the way to Indonesia or even Australia? And what about Africa? Would he have stretched his empire to encompass modern-day West Africa all the way to the Atlantic? We can only speculate, of course.

There are plenty of holes in the story of Alexander, mainly because most of the immediate sources are lost forever to time itself. But even the precious little information we have today at our disposal tells us more than enough. It tells us a tale of one man who would become the single most prominent figure of Europe in early antiquity, perhaps only overshadowed by the many Roman generals and statesmen, with Gaius Julius Caesar front and center. A tale of a man who followed in the footsteps of his father and turned an impossible dream into reality, having shed the blood of millions and risking dozens of friendships to do so.

Here's another book by Captivating History that you might like

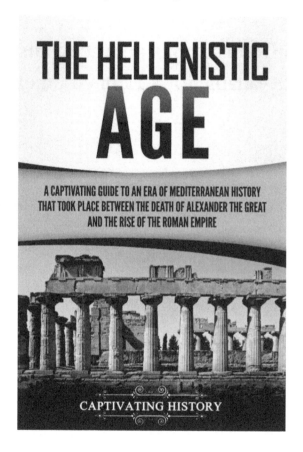

Free Bonus from Captivating History (Available for a Limited time)

Hi History Lovers!

Now you have a chance to join our exclusive history list so you can get your first history ebook for free as well as discounts and a potential to get more history books for free! Simply visit the link below to join.

Captivatinghistory.com/ebook

Also, make sure to follow us on Facebook, Twitter and Youtube by searching for Captivating History.

Bibliography and References

Badian, E. (1958): Alexander the Great and the Unity of Mankind, In *Historia: Zeitschrift für Alte Geschichte,* Vol. 7, No. 4, (pp. 425-444). Stuttgart, Germany: Franz Steiner Verlag.

Bieber, M. (1949): The Portraits of Alexander the Great, In *Proceedings of the American Philosophical Society,* Vol. 93, No. 5, (pp. 373-421 & 423-427). Philadelphia, PA, USA: American Philosophical Society.

Burn, A. R. (1956): *Alexander the Great and the Hellenistic Empire.* London, UK: English Universities Press Ltd.

Cartledge, P. (2004): *Alexander the Great: The Truth behind the Myth,* New York, NY, USA: The Overlook Press.

Encyclopedia Britannica (1981), Retrieved on April 15th 2021, from https://www.britannica.com.

Green, P. (2007): *Alexander the Great and the Hellenistic Age.* London, UK: Weidenfeld and Nicholson.

Heckel, W. (1998): *The Wars of Alexander the Great.* London, UK: Osprey Publishing.

J. W. McCrindle (1969): *The Invasion of India By Alexander the Great: As Described by Arrian, Q. Curtius, Diodoros Plutarch and Justin.* New York, NY, USA: Barnes & Noble.

Merlan, P. (1954): Isocrates, Aristotle and Alexander the Great, In *Historia: Zeitschrift für Alte Geschichte,* Vol. 3, No. 1, (pp. 60-81). Stuttgart, Germany: Franz Steiner Verlag.

Secunda, N. & Warry, J. (1998): *Alexander the Great: His Armies and Campaigns 334-323 BC.* London, UK: Osprey Publishing.

Stoneman, R. (1991). *The Greek Alexander Romance.* London, UK: Penguin.

Thomas, K. R. (1995): A psychoanalytic study of Alexander the Great, In *The Psychoanalytic Review* Vol. 82, No. 6, (pp. 859-901). New York, NY, USA: Guilford Press.

Wikipedia (January 15, 2001), Retrieved on April 15th 2021, from www.wikipedia.org/.

Notes on Images

[1] b

Made in the USA
Las Vegas, NV
25 May 2022

49365160R00069